LIVING WITH
MID-CENTURY
COLLECTIBLES

LIVING WITH
MID-CENTURY
COLLECTIBLES

CLASSIC PIECES FROM THE BIRTH
OF CONTEMPORARY DESIGN

DOMINIC LUTYENS

LONDON · NEW YORK

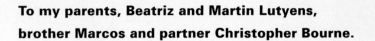

To my parents, Beatriz and Martin Lutyens, brother Marcos and partner Christopher Bourne.

Senior designer Paul Tilby
Commissioning editor
Annabel Morgan
Picture research Christina Borsi
Production manager
Gordana Simakovic
Art director Leslie Harrington
Editorial director Julia Charles

First published in 2013
by Ryland Peters & Small
20–21 Jockey's Fields,
London WC1R 4BW
and
519 Broadway, 5th Floor
New York, NY 10012
www.rylandpeters.com

10 9 8 7 6 5 4 3 2 1

Text © Dominic Lutyens 2013
Design and commissioned
photography © Ryland Peters &
Small 2013

ISBN 978 1 84975 448 4

A catalogue record for this book is
available from the British Library.

US Library of Congress cataloging-
in-publication data has been
applied for.

Printed and bound in China

INTRODUCTION

Mid-century design is an umbrella term for a period that has its roots in the mid-1930s and peaked in the mid-1960s.

Arguably, it continued – albeit falteringly – until the 1973 oil crisis, which made it too expensive to produce the plastic, space-age furniture that was its last incarnation.

Yet mid-century design, now abbreviated by fans to the snappier 'mid-century', is fantastically popular today. Its boxy, low-slung sideboards, bulbous glassware, jazzy abstract textiles and contour-cradling armchairs grace hip homes, boutique hotels and designer stores the world over.

Mid-century was a development of the forbiddingly severe, mainly monochrome, geometric, early 20th-century modernist design created by the Bauhaus in Germany. But early modernism's narrowly prescriptive, form-follows-function credo – fuelled by an obsession with the machine age – began to evolve, by the late 1930s, into the more forgiving aesthetic of mid-century, which embraced gracefully curvilinear, more ergonomic, often asymmetric forms and joyous colour and pattern.

This shift was pioneered in the 1920s by Finnish architect and designer Alvar Aalto, who patented a technique for wood-bending in 1932, which resulted in his bent plywood armchair of the same year – a hit at the 1939 New York World's Fair. Aalto's organic

ABOVE This 1960 Ox chair is by Hans Wegner, one of Denmark's most prominent mid-century designers.

RIGHT A 1950s dining table and chairs by British designer TH Robsjohn-Gibbings, who later worked for Widdicomb, a US manufacturer of mid-century furniture.

OPPOSITE These chairs – called Antony after a student hall of residence in Antony near Paris for which they were made – and the table are by French designer Jean Prouvé. He co-created the 1950s bookshelf behind with Charlotte Perriand.

designs sprang both from technological advances and from the inspiration he took from nature, namely Finland's untamed landscapes. Prewar modernist art inspired him, too – the biomorphic motifs of Jean Arp's wooden relief sculptures were echoed in Aalto's furniture – as it did much mid-century design, which proliferated chiefly in the US, UK, Italy and Scandinavia.

Despite their differences, mid-century and early 20th-century modernist designers shared a belief that good design should be available to all. 'After the war, a lot of designers in the UK had Left-leaning sympathies and a vision of a more socially equitable Britain,' says design and applied arts journalist Corinne Julius, whose parents' London-based firm Hille manufactured uncompromisingly modernist furniture. 'They believed good design could improve people's lives.'

Postwar, many countries set out to reconstruct themselves, and contemporary design – craved by an increasingly affluent public – played a key role in this. Meanwhile, new technologies and materials led to the creation of increasingly innovative pieces.

Mid-century design was at once a global and a local phenomenon. Its ideas were widely disseminated by international design fairs and by avant-garde European designers who emigrated from Germany in the 1930s to the US. According to Simon Andrews, director of 20th Century Decorative Art & Design at Christie's, London, American GIs also helped to spread the word after the war: 'Having fought in France and Italy, they

Multi-purpose storage was a major mid-century trend. Alvar Aalto's 1937 Tea Trolley (above) doubled as a storage unit. But it was US designer George Nelson's 1959 Comprehensive Storage System (top right) that truly pioneered this vogue.

OPPOSITE **Hans Wegner's 1950 Flag Halyard chair referenced the early modernists' obsession with tubular-steel frames, but chimed with mid-century's love of indulgently comfortable chairs.**

returned home with a much more cosmopolitan taste for the fashion and design they'd seen in Paris or Rome.'

Some countries, however, were associated with certain national aesthetics: Italy was renowned for its flamboyant colours and forms; Denmark for handcrafted, simple, wooden furniture, and as such with understated 'good taste'.

In fact, the enduring popularity of mid-century is down to it being so culturally rich and multifaceted. 'It represents one of the most fascinating chapters in the history of design,' says Simon Andrews. 'It gave people the first opportunity to engage with modernism on a democratic level. It was honest – these objects spoke eloquently and humbly of their function. And there are so many strands to it: it references everything from fine art to space-age style.'

TIMELINE: MID-CENTURY MILESTONES

1932

PAIMIO ARMCHAIR
Alvar Aalto

Finnish architect and designer Alvar Aalto (1898–1976) once observed that modernist, tubular-steel furniture was 'unsatisfactory from a human point of view'. The visionary Aalto proceeded to experiment with more ergonomic alternatives, including his revolutionary Paimio armchair for his building the Paimio Sanatorium (a hospital for tuberculosis patients) of 1929–1933. Comprising a laminated birch frame and bent ply seat, it heralded mid-century's organic aesthetic.

1934

STANDARD CHAIR
Jean Prouvé

Designer and architect Jean Prouvé (1901–1984) grew up in Nancy, France, among its artistic community, L'Ecole de Nancy, which strove to make art accessible and forge links between art and industry. Prouvé deployed mass-production techniques in his own avant-garde Standard chair, whose steel back legs take most of the strain from the sitter's upper-body weight, allowing for comparatively delicate front legs. Marrying metal with more organic-looking wood, it represents a radical departure from early modernist, tubular-steel furniture.

1934

WORKING CHAIR
Bruno Mathsson

Aalto's experiments with ergonomic design were echoed – and extended – by Sweden's Bruno Mathsson (1907–1988) when he created his Working chair (now called Eva chair), whose bentwood frame and innovative webbing seat accommodates the human body comfortably. It was an early example of 'Swedish Modern', a term coined in the 1930s when modern Swedish design began to wow Europe and the US.

1937

AMERICAN MODERN DINNERWARE

Russel Wright

Radically biomorphic forms were also a hallmark of this dinnerware by American industrial designer Russel Wright (1904–1976) for the Steubenville Pottery in Ohio. Wright promoted the idea of informal living, and this best-selling dinnerware's other innovation is its flexibility: available in a spectrum of complementary colours, its different pieces can be mixed and matched.

1938

SOFT FORMS TABLEWARE

Wilhelm Kåge

The organic aesthetic adopted by modernist designers in the 1930s was manifested in ceramics, thanks also to the Soft Forms tableware of Swedish-born Wilhelm Kåge (1889–1960) for porcelain factory Gustavsberg. This teamed pared-down forms with curvaceous, sometimes eccentrically wobbly contours.

1946

KANTARELLI VASE

Tapio Wirkkala

Nature hugely influenced mid-century design but was often represented in an abstracted, stylized way. A seminal example is the sensually curvilinear, ambiguous Kantarelli vase by Finland's Tapio Wirkkala (1915–1985), a multitalented designer who also created banknotes and ceramics. *Kantarelli* means 'chanterelle mushroom', and the vase evokes this obliquely via finely engraved lines that allude to the ribbing on the mushroom's underside.

1948

LA CHAISE CHAIR
Charles and Ray Eames

The outlandishly organic, apparently amorphous shape of the La Chaise chair by Charles Eames (1907–1978) and his wife Ray (1912–1988) prefigured the playfully asymmetric, sculptural forms of much mid-century design. Yet its upholstery-free fibreglass seat is more practical than whimsical: its anthropomorphic shape allows the user to sit *and* recline. It was designed for the competition, Low-Cost Furniture Design organized by The Museum of Modern Art, New York, and was inspired by sculptor Gaston Lachaise.

1952

ANT CHAIR
Arne Jacobsen

Designed by Arne Jacobsen (1902–1971) for the canteen of Danish pharmaceutical firm Novo Nordisk, this stackable, best-selling design for Fritz Hansen was named after its similarity to an ant's silhouette, and demonstrates nature's enormous influence on mid-century design. Jacobsen said it was also inspired by Charles and Ray Eames's moulded plywood furniture.

1957

SUPERLEGGERA CHAIR
Gio Ponti

In contrast to strictly forward-looking modernist designers, Gio Ponti (1891–1979) fused a modern aesthetic with craft traditions. With its skeletal ash frame and Indian cane seat, this 1.7 kg (3¾ lb) chair for Cassina (*superleggera* means 'super-light' in Italian) was inspired by Italy's slender but robust 19th-century Chiavari chairs. It was at the vanguard of the mid-century vogue for light, transparent furniture, and can be lifted by a child using one finger.

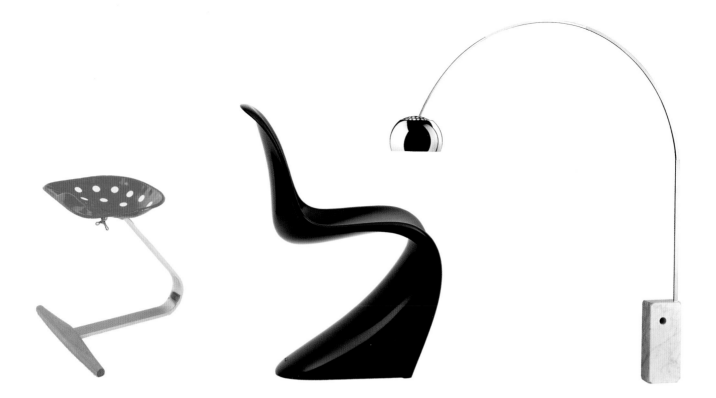

1957

MEZZADRO STOOL

Achille and Pier Giacomo Castiglioni

One mid-century innovation was to introduce industrial, mass-produced elements into the domestic sphere, as Italian designer Achille Castiglioni (1918–2002) and his brother Pier Giacomo (1913–1968) did with their cutting-edge Mezzadro stool. Its ready-made, mass-produced tractor seat also gives a nod to avant-garde artist Marcel Duchamp's use of ready-mades (found objects) in his work. Mezzadro wasn't put into production until 1971, by Italian brand Zanotta.

1960

PANTON CHAIR OR S CHAIR

Verner Panton

The highly experimental Danish-born designer Verner Panton (1926–1998) is perhaps best-known for his Panton chair, the world's first seat made of one piece of injection-moulded plastic. Amalgamating legs, seat and backrest in its sinuous, high-gloss, proto-Pop form, it was inspired by Panton's visit to a factory that made plastic safety helmets and buckets. Technical difficulties delayed its manufacture; it was finally put into production by Vitra in 1967.

1962

ARCO LIGHT

Achille and Pier Giacomo Castiglioni

Typically influenced by industrial design – in this case, a street light – the Castiglioni brothers created the Arco lamp, a highly original hybrid of a floor and pendant lamp, for Italian lighting firm Flos. The vaulting lamp gracefully swoops 2.5m (8ft) across a room to illuminate sofas or tables. The hole in the lamp's heavy marble base allows for a broom handle to be inserted in it so that it can be lifted and moved easily.

THE
MID-CENTURY
LOOK

Mid-century design is more complex than it appears – and the more fascinating for it. A double-edged movement, it was inspired by nature yet was made possible by advances in technology. Progressive politics and an optimism about the future after the war sparked an enthusiasm for colour, pattern and new, sensual shapes. This chapter unpicks the many strands of this richly variegated period of design.

Arne Jacobsen's graceful 1958 Swan chair alluded to nature, yet its representation of a swan was abstracted and stylized.

RIGHT A seminal example of organic modernism, a style that emerged in the 1940s, was Eero Saarinen's 1946 Womb chair. He was worried that its name might cause offence but kept it. 'I've been thinking about a more printable name, but my mind keeps turning to something more biological,' he said.

BELOW RIGHT Danish designer Børge Mogensen's 1958 Spanish chair reveals his taste for the organic aesthetic via his choice of wood and leather. It was inspired by a trip to Andalusia, Spain.

NATURE

The influence of nature – and Art Nouveau – on early 20th-century architects, such as Frank Lloyd Wright, whose building Fallingwater in rural Pennsylvania jutted over a waterfall, had been suppressed by the machine-worshipping early modernists. But if they favoured rectilinear shapes over Art Nouveau's wayward, tendril-like forms, by the 1940s avant-garde designers and architects – following Alvar Aalto's lead – embraced organic forms afresh. Eero Saarinen's 1962 TWA Flight Center terminal at New York's JFK airport resembled a swooping bird, and mid-century architects' houses beckoned the great outdoors in via gigantic sliding windows. In the UK in the 1950s, many consumers sought an antidote to the severe aesthetic

of rationed utility furniture and hankered after softer, organic forms.

The influence of nature wasn't unconscious. Indeed, the term 'organic' was officially adopted to describe an emerging aesthetic primarily inspired by avant-garde sculpture. In the US, it was spearheaded by Charles Eames and Eero Saarinen. From 1937 to 1940, Eames headed the design department at the Cranbrook Academy of Art, near Detroit, where he befriended Saarinen and artist

and designer Ray Kaiser, whom Eames married in 1941 and who closely collaborated with him. In 1940, the Museum of Modern Art in New York (MoMA) held a design competition entitled Organic Design in Home Furnishings, which defined design as organic 'if, within the object as a whole, there is a harmonious relationship between the individual elements as regards structure, material and purpose'. The judges included Aalto, who had exhibited a plywood chair at MoMA in 1938.

ABOVE **A pioneer of the American 'studio furniture' movement, Japanese-American designer George Nakashima made tables hewn out of raw wood that represented organic modernism at its most extreme, authentic and romantic. Nakashima was held in an internment camp in the US after the attack on Pearl Harbor, and later moved to Pennsylvania where he made his wood furniture.**

LEFT AND OPPOSITE ABOVE **Mainstream crockery often pictured a domesticated version of nature, as these 1950s plates by Terence Conran for UK manufacturer Midwinter show. One (left), called Plantlife, features a fabulously '50s Swiss cheese plant; the other (opposite), Nature Study, stylized dragonflies and moths.**

OPPOSITE, BOTTOM **Finland's Timo Sarpaneva used moulds made of charred bark to create glassware that directly evoked the natural world.**

Eames, assisted by Ray and in collaboration with Saarinen, won two first prizes, one of them for a moulded plywood seat. In 1941, the Eameses moved to Los Angeles, where they began developing a process for 3D moulding of plywood that resulted in the creation of many organic designs. The same year, the taste for the organic was further consolidated by MoMA's exhibition Organic Design in Home Furnishings.

This new style may not have made direct references to nature, but its influence could be felt in the gently rounded forms and use of natural materials evident in the work of Eames and myriad mid-century designers.

Even so, organic design wasn't always made of natural materials and could be classed as such simply by alluding to natural or biological forms: Saarinen's Womb chair of 1946 is fashioned out of fibreglass and tubular steel, while his Tulip chair of 1956 shoots upwards on a single, flower-like 'stem' rather than four legs.

In Sweden, Denmark and Finland, whose governments championed the furniture industry, wood was widely used by designers such as Denmark's Hans Wegner and Finn Juhl and

Finland's Ilmari Tapiovaara to make impeccably crafted furniture.

Meanwhile, Finland's Timo Sarpaneva and Tapio Wirkkala produced rough-textured glassware for Finnish company Iittala that overtly evoked the country's landscapes – its craggy rocks, ice and bark. One of Wirkkala's most iconic pieces was his 1946 Kantarelli vase, named after the chanterelle mushroom, while one of Sarpaneva's best-known designs is his ultra-sculptural Orchid vase of 1953.

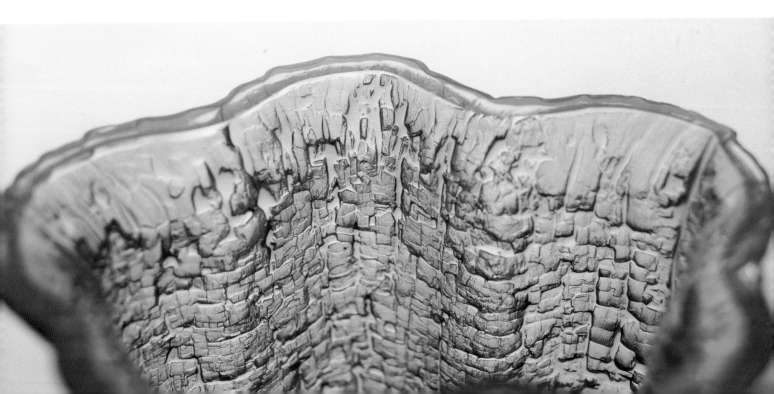

Like their close collaborator Eero Saarinen, the Eameses – co-creators of their LCW chair, seen in close-up here – developed multilayered veneers in ash, walnut or birch that could be moulded into complex curves, which made the 1930s experiments with bent-ply furniture look tame and two-dimensional by comparison.

ABOVE Hans Wegner generally favoured traditional wood, but his 1950 Flag Halyard chair nods to technology with its back and seat made of a utilitarian, ready-made material – sailing rope – bound tightly around its steel frame.

ABOVE Ernest Race's Antelope chair highlights his talent for manipulating thin metal rods to create skeletal but robust cast-aluminium furniture in gracefully curvaceous shapes. It won a silver medal at the 1954 Milan Triennale.

ABOVE The Eameses' 1956 Lounge Chair and Ottoman shows their mastery of moulding plywood. The duo constantly exploited new industrial processes, such as 'cycle-welding', which enabled wood to be joined to rubber, glass and metal.

TECHNOLOGY

Ironically, organic design – furniture in particular – frequently relied on the latest technology to achieve its innovative, often irregular forms. And technology was welcomed for social reasons: many mid-century designers, chiefly in the US, allied themselves to mass-production, believing it democratized design by making it more affordable.

During World War II, wood-bending techniques became more sophisticated. Experiments with materials carried out by the automotive and aeronautical industries during the war were exploited by designers, most famously by the Eameses. After making their moulded plywood pieces, they created fibreglass-reinforced chair seats under which were rubber discs called shock mounts that absorbed the impact of the metal legs on the fibreglass – a wartime innovation. Increasingly narrow gauges of steel were also available, and used to make spindly yet strong chair legs.

In the postwar years, new, lightweight materials, notably plastics, took experimentation to unprecedented extremes. In Italy – whose cutting-edge designs began to challenge the dominance of its US counterparts – designers avidly investigated the possibilities of these new materials. In 1950, designer Marco Zanuso created his Lady chair of 1951 using Pirelli's latest innovation – foam rubber. And in the 1960s, injection-moulding techniques allowed designers to create plastic furniture in almost any shape.

MOULDED WOOD

Danish designer Poul Kjaerholm's black lacquered, bent plywood PK0 chair of 1952. In 1958, Kjaerholm showed his work at an influential exhibition called Formes Scandinaves in Paris. He also won the Grand Prix at the Milan Triennale in 1957 and 1960.

OPPOSITE, INSET **Alvar Aalto's Lounge Chair 400 of 1936 has bent wood arms that curve to form a frame for the chair.**

ABOVE **UK manufacturer Ercol's 1958 Butterfly chair is constructed of bent laminated wood.**

ABOVE RIGHT **Aalto made huge strides in his experiments with moulded plywood with his furniture for his architectural projects, the Viipuri Library of 1927 and Paimio Sanatorium of 1929, for which he created his iconic Paimio armchair.**

Technological advances were the bedrock of early modernist design, and a key innovation was the moulding and bending of wood. A seminal example was cabinetmaker Michael Thonet's experiments with steam-bending wood that spawned his best-selling bentwood No 14 chair in 1859.

Aalto's wood-bending, which exemplified the unlikely alliance of technology and organic design that lies at the root of mid-century design, was more sophisticated yet still necessitated arduous manual work. Aalto began his research into moulding plywood in the 1920s, working with his wife Aino, then with Otto Korhonen, a manager at carpentry workshop Huonekalu-ja Rakennustyötehdas, which fabricated Aalto's chairs for the Paimio Sanatorium. These combined sherry-pale, laminated birch arms and legs that form a continuous, sinuous line with an undulating seat and back in thinner birch ply. The chairs' angle, which allowed patients sitting on them to breathe more easily, even had health benefits. Aalto patented his wood-moulding technique in 1933, the same year he designed his equally acclaimed bent-ply, stackable Stool 60 and showcased his furniture at the exhibition Wood Only held at Fortnum & Mason in London.

LEFT Danish designers Peter Hvidt and Orla Mølgaard-Nielsen, who formed a long-standing partnership in 1944, created their best-known piece, the AX chair, in 1947. The curved, laminated wood chair was manufactured by Fritz Hansen.

OPPOSITE The US architect and designer Norman Cherner's generously curvaceous, bent plywood Cherner chair of 1958 was originally made by the Massachusetts-based manufacturer Plycraft and remained in production until the 1970s. In 1999, his two sons reissued the chair and other designs by their father.

Aalto's influence was evident in Marcel Breuer's chaise longue created for Frank Pritchard's British firm the Isokon Furniture Company, established in 1935. This also manufactured Egon Riis's bent-ply Penguin Donkey bookcase.

Another watershed in this technology came during World War II when the aeronautical industry developed new synthetic resins used for bonding laminates that made them stronger, while wood could be bent using electrical machinery. During the war, the Eameses furiously experimented with bending plywood into 3D shapes in a spare bedroom of their LA home, using a makeshift press they dubbed their 'Kazam! machine', after the saying 'ala kazam', because the plywood and glue fed into it moulded into the desired shapes like magic. In 1941, the Eameses produced moulded plywood splints for wounded servicemen for the US Navy, later creating their so-called 'plywood group' of furniture, including the LCW chair of 1945 and dining chair version called DCW, all manufactured by US firm Herman Miller. They continued this theme with their Lounge Chair and Ottoman of 1956, whose frame, made of moulded plywood veneered with rosewood, encased luxuriously supple, black leather upholstery.

Successors of the moulded plywood furniture of Aalto and the Eameses include Arne Jacobsen's Ant chair and Norman Cherner's 1957 Cherner chair with its extravagantly looping bentwood arms.

WIRE-ROD AND METAL

The Eameses were pioneers of another postwar technological leap – wire-rod furniture, which took off with the advent of new, super-narrow yet strong gauges of steel. While these gave designers a gratifyingly malleable material to play with, wire-rod furniture appealed, too, for aesthetic reasons: transparent and unimposing, it perfectly complemented uncluttered, open-plan, mid-century interiors. A buzzword then was 'casual living' and lightweight wire-mesh chairs were also coveted for being easy to move about.

A seminal example of wire-rod furniture was the Eameses' DAR chair – standing for 'dining armchair rod' – put into production in 1950 by Herman Miller. 'Rod' referred to the metal, pylon-like struts of its intricate yet skeletal legs. Hinting at engineering, these were aptly named after the Eiffel Tower.

Some have speculated that artist Alberto Giacometti's elongated bronze sculptures influenced wire-rod furniture. In fact, its other main exponent was sculptor Harry Bertoia, who emigrated from his native Italy to the US in the 1930s. After collaborating with the Eameses, he designed his classic, sculptural, wire-mesh Diamond and Bird chairs, produced by US furniture manufacturer Knoll in 1952. Bertoia was delighted that they were so transparent as to be almost dematerialized: 'The chairs are studies in space, form and metal… They are mostly made of air, like a sculpture. Space passes straight through them,' he rhapsodized.

Meanwhile, Verner Panton dreamt up his lattice-tastic Wire Cone chair in 1958, while Warren Platner created chairs made by welding hundreds of steel rods to circular frames for Knoll in 1966.

OPPOSITE LEFT The Eameses' insatiable appetite for exploring new materials led them to design their Wire Mesh chair in 1951, soon after making their first moulded plastic chairs in the '40s. It sometimes came with a seat and back pad, earning it the catchy nickname 'the bikini'.

OPPOSITE RIGHT With their starker, straight-edged, vertical arrangement of parallel steel rods, Warren Platner's 1725 chairs, tables and stools differed from the Eameses' and Harry Bertoia's chairs, whose grids of bent wire were softer, curvier and mesh-like.

THIS PAGE Harry Bertoia's classic chairs for Knoll. These were an instant commercial hit, allowing him to concentrate on his main passion – sculpture.

MOULDED PLASTIC

The Eameses experimented with moulded plastic furniture in the 1940s – their DAR chair had a plastic seat – but their breakthrough was modest compared with innovations in plastics in the 1950s, '60s and '70s. While DAR comprised a separate plastic seat and metal legs, a new, far greater challenge was to create furniture from a single material – plastic.

Eero Saarinen aimed to do this with his 1950s Tulip chairs. 'The undercarriage of chairs... in a typical interior makes an ugly, confusing, unrestful world,' he lamented. 'I wanted to clear up the slum of legs... make the chair all one thing again.' Alas, the limitations of 1950s plastics technology meant that Saarinen had to settle for a chair in two parts – a moulded fibreglass seat and an aluminium leg with a plastic finish. Injection-moulded plastics

enabled Panton to achieve Saarinen's elusive goal and create his ground-breaking, single-piece, injection-moulded plastic Panton chair.

Many shared Panton's passion for plastic and its appealingly slick, homogeneous surface. Yrjö Kukkapuro's Karuselli chair of 1963 – its shape apparently inspired by the impression he made in the snow on returning home after a drunken night out – has an enormous fibreglass seat. Eero Aarnio's ultra-space age Ball chair of the same year comprises a simple globe sliced at an angle to provide a fully upholstered interior and seat. Joe Colombo's 1965 Universale chair and 1970 Boby trolley were made of injection-moulded ABS plastic, whose rainbow-bright hues signalled the collision of mid-century design and the pop-cum-space-age aesthetic.

[OPPOSITE] **Paradoxically, many designers were drawn to plastics, as they could be sculpted into organic, smooth-contoured furniture, like Finnish designer Yrjö Kukkapuro's swivelling, rocking Karuselli chair. 'A chair should be softly shaped like people are,' he once said.**

[OPPOSITE, INSET] **Fellow Finn Eero Aarnio's uber-pop, fibreglass 1967 Pastil seat. His first fibreglass design was his 1963 Ball chair. A later variant of it was his groovy 1968 ceiling-hung Bubble chair.**

[RIGHT] **Eero Saarinen's Tulip chairs. Saarinen's holy grail in the 1950s was to make furniture out of a single piece of plastic, but the technological limitations of the time thwarted him.**

THIS PAGE AND OPPOSITE **The Eameses' moulded plastic DAR chair was submitted to MoMA's Low-Cost Furniture competition of 1948. Pointing out later that it was the first piece of furniture made of fibreglass-reinforced plastic, the museum also extolled its smooth surface, virtual indestructibility and flexible design demonstrated by its variety of bases – one of these resulting in this RAR rocker. The duo's 1948 La Chaise chaise longue (opposite) was similarly versatile.**

OPPOSITE Postwar design's more inclusive aesthetic gave creatives carte blanche to develop a personal, even idiosyncratic style. Experimenting with forms – from ruggedly textured, bark-like glass and stylized, mushroom-shaped lighting to molecular motifs, reflecting a burgeoning curiosity for science – was one way to do so.

RIGHT Statement-making lounge chairs – often originally created by architects to furnish their avant-garde buildings – were another expression of this greater freedom. Many were named after the shapes they formed, giving rise to such self-explanatory designs as Verner Panton's Heart chair and Pierre Paulin's Tongue seat.

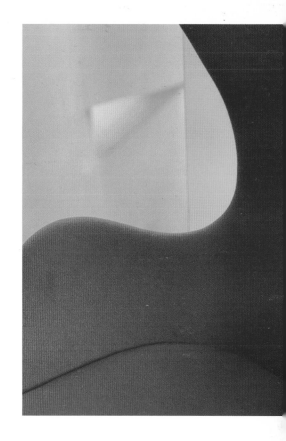

SHAPES

T he rejection by mid-century creatives of the functionalist credo of early modernism gave them unbridled freedom to experiment with expressive forms in all areas of design. A typical example of this shift in taste is US-based Eva Zeisel's zany, bulbous, even protoplasmic 1940s Town and Country tableware (see page 131). Zeisel herself pronounced, 'Form does not follow function'. In particular, products that weren't mass-produced, such as hand-made ceramics and glass, adopted wildly sculptural, asymmetrical, often irrational forms.

Inspirations came from everywhere, from art to fashion. In her book *The New Look: Design in the Fifties*, Lesley Jackson argued that mid-century's love of hourglass forms was influenced by Christian Dior's New Look of 1947.

Modernist art's predilection, post-Cubism, for abstract, amorphous, asymmetric forms was also hugely influential. While Aalto's furniture channelled Jean Arp's amoeboid sculptures, much mid-century design took the form of Joan Miró's leitmotifs – crescents, kidneys, antennae. After seeing an exhibition on Jackson Pollock at London's Whitechapel Gallery in 1958, British metalworker Robert Welch made a candelabrum mimicking Pollock's visceral drip paintings.

In Italy, where small-volume production was common and self-expression prized, design often resembled art. Italian ceramicist Antonia Campi, for example, produced a vase influenced by Yves Tanguy's Surrealist paintings.

ABOVE Many designers, such as Robert Welch, who created this Jackson Pollock-inspired candelabrum, related to abstract and Surrealist art. Both movements were appealingly modern and encouraged the self-expression designers also cultivated.

LEFT Forward-thinking UK company Poole Pottery produced these sinuous bowls in the 1950s and '60s.

BELOW Organic ceramics were pioneered in Sweden by Wilhelm Kåge with his Soft Forms tableware for Gustavsberg, where he was art director before handing the reins to Stig Lindberg, who made this 1950s Veckla bowl. The Swedish ceramicist Gunnar Nylund created the shapely vases.

OPPOSITE The names of Arne Jacobsen's Swan chair on the left and George Nelson's Coconut chair, right, make their organic inspirations plain.

ORGANIC

Fluid and unpredictable, organic forms appealed in particular, as these could adopt any shape designers desired – and looked ultra-modern. Their popularity opened the floodgates for the creation of unapologetically idiosyncratic pieces.

According to Simon Andrews, director of 20th Century Decorative Art and Design at Christie's, London, the vogue for organic shapes represented a backlash against angular early modernism: 'All fashions reflect a pendulum swing. Mid-century designers were reacting against the Viennese design group Wiener Werkstätte and the Bauhaus's tubular-steel furniture.' Even so, like early modernism, organic modernism, whose free-form shapes were usually simple and stylized, favoured pared-down forms. These are also described as biomorphic – meaning a decorative object resembling a living organism – as is the art of Arp, Miró, Henry Moore and Barbara Hepworth.

Mid-century furniture often looked organic and curvilinear for a practical reason: it was more comfortable and ergonomic. Its curves also mirrored the trend for greater informality and lounging. Eero Saarinen's Womb chair (see page 19) – so-called because you could curl up in it – was conceived after

Florence Knoll, furniture designer and co-founder of Knoll Associates, remarked that she was 'sick of those chairs that hold you in one position'.

Meanwhile, 1950s design was often inspired by plants, notably tulips (also the word for Saarinen's chairs and tables) and animals. Swedish glassworks Orrefors produced Nils Landberg's Tulip vase and Ingeborg Lundin's Apple vase (see page 135). Denmark's Per Lütken named some of his work – like his Duckling vase of 1950 for Danish glass company Holmegaard – after animals, while architect and designer Arne Jacobsen called the chairs he created for the SAS Royal Hotel in Copenhagen Egg and Swan, thereby spelling out their organic provenance. And insect legs inspired another mid-century mannerism – all things spindly and tapered.

OPPOSITE US-based Vladimir Kagan's 1950s Floating Curve sofa and Sculptured coffee table typify his organic furniture with a strongly theatrical flavour.

OPPOSITE ABOVE RIGHT Other US designers, such as TH Robsjohn-Gibbings who created this table, Phillip Lloyd Powell and Paul McCobb, made wood-based furniture that dovetailed with this movement.

ABOVE With New York's MoMA championing organic modernism, it's not surprising that many US furniture designers created pieces in this style. Its 1940 competition with this theme helped make stars of the Eameses, creators of their Lounge Chair and Ottoman.

RIGHT Similarly organic are Isamu Noguchi's iconic coffee table and a collection of Scandinavian glass.

While Arne Jacobsen's furniture was opulently curvilinear, his metalware, such as his 1960s stainless steel Cylinda-Line tableware for Copenhagen-based Stelton, was sleek, geometric and minimalist.

GEOMETRIC

Given their weakness for organic forms, mid-century designers rarely produced geometric pieces. However, the movement was so eclectic that some designers and manufacturers created angular, minimalist homeware. Occasionally, designers harked back to the more playful, colourful elements of early modernism, notably the furniture of Gerrit Rietveld and canvases of Piet Mondrian, both members of the Dutch artistic movement De Stijl. In 1949, the Eameses developed their Mondrian-esque ESU shelving unit, whose industrial aesthetic of primary-coloured panels and almost Lego-like moulded plywood broadcast their love of mass-production.

Knoll Associates, co-founded by German-born, US-based Hans Knoll and his wife Florence in New York in 1946, produced highly geometric pieces, including her boxy, button-backed Lounge chair on square chrome legs. This recalled architect Mies van der Rohe's Barcelona chair, which was designed to complement the sharply geometric planes of his German Pavilion at the Barcelona International Exhibition of 1929. In fact, Knoll, which held the rights to make pieces by former Bauhaus luminaries van der Rohe and Marcel Breuer – who had taught Florence at the Cranbrook Academy – represented a continuation of, rather than a break from, early modernism.

In the 1960s, design in general became more geometric and minimalist, a prime example being

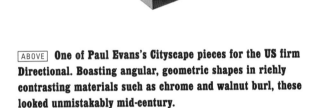

ABOVE One of Paul Evans's Cityscape pieces for the US firm Directional. Boasting angular, geometric shapes in richly contrasting materials such as chrome and walnut burl, these looked unmistakably mid-century.

BELOW Florence Knoll's ultra-geometric, Mies van der Rohe-influenced Lounge chair and sofa of 1954 for Knoll.

that mid-century staple, the crisply rectilinear sideboard – from Florence Knoll's Credenza of 1961 to Stag and G-Plan's versions. Similarly straight-edged were US designer Paul Evans's 1960s Cityscape sideboards and dining tables, which evoked modernist architecture. More stripped down still was Arne Jacobsen's stainless steel Cylinda-Line tableware for Stelton.

GRAPHIC AND LINEAR

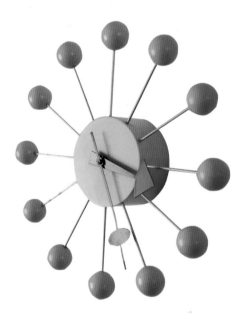

nother stylistic tic of 1950s design was super-fine, linear patterns on ceramics and textiles. These looked hand-drawn, tentative and delicate, and so inevitably brought to mind fine art and illustration.

This trend was also evident in some furniture and lighting, whose linear quality made them look more 2D than 3D. Take Cees Braakman's SM05 steel-wire chair for Dutch company Pastoe in 1958 (see page 77). And the Eameses' DKX Wire chairs of 1951 were pictured on the cover of *The Architectural Review* the following year in silhouette, which highlighted their linear, graphic quality. Similarly linear was British designer Ernest Race's Antelope chair (see page 80), designed for the Festival of Britain. Held in the UK in 1951, this was organized by the government to create a feeling of recovery after the war and promote Britain's contribution to science and the arts. Naturally, the skinny legs of Arne Jacobsen's Ant chair simulate those of the insect it's named after.

Equally insect-like were French designer Serge Mouille's beanpole-slim metal lights of the 1950s. His articulated, kinetic lamps – they can be swung to face different directions – were painted black, accentuating their graphic look. These have been compared to the mobiles of artist Alexander Calder, which also influenced a textile created in 1954 by June Lyon for London shop Heal's, one of very few British stores to stock mid-century in the 1950s. It was for Heal's, too, that Lucienne Day, one of the most influential textile designers of the period, created her 1950s Calyx (see page 56) and Graphica fabrics dominated by spidery lines. Day took inspiration from artist Paul Klee, whose paintings often had a linear element. Another design in this vein is Terence Conran's Chequers tableware of 1957 for Midwinter, decorated with a grid of childlike pencil lines.

[ABOVE TOP] **Britain's cutting-edge textiles manufacturer David Whitehead produced this strongly linear design with an exploding, fractal pattern. It's very possible that it channelled avant-garde art, since the firm made textiles by Henry Moore and John Piper.**

[ABOVE] **George Nelson's stripped-down, linear, funky 1949 Ball clock for US firm Howard Miller Clock Company. Its ball-tipped spokes simultaneously nodded to a science-inspired vogue for molecular motifs. Equally graphic was Nelson's black Asterisk clock.**

[OPPOSITE] **Serge Mouille's skeletal luminaires were similarly linear and graphic.**

OPPOSITE A 1950s Danish two-seater sofa combines the wood frame typical of Danish mid-century design with upholstered backs and seats in a zingy peacock blue shade.

RIGHT A vibrantly upholstered Jacobsen Swan chair and Freeform sofa, designed by Isamu Noguchi in 1946. After the war, many mid-century designers and manufacturers hankered after colour as much as consumers who had been woefully deprived of it during the '40s, especially in countries severely affected by austerity.

COLOURS

In those countries directly affected by World War II, and during the austerity years that followed, people were starved of colour. Design and decoration were largely superfluous to the war effort, and 1940s colours were drab and utilitarian. All this changed in the 1950s. In the UK, the Festival of Britain, which attracted over 10 million visitors, transformed the country's visual landscape, according to design and applied arts journalist Corinne Julius, who was a child in the 1950s: 'During the '40s, there wasn't the money for colour and it didn't seem appropriate. I don't think anyone who's not of my generation can understand how dull and grey everything had been. The Festival of Britain was really exciting. It brought this burst of colour.'

The US came out of the war relatively unscathed and was comparatively prosperous, yet its manufacturers also splurged on colour. Knoll and Herman Miller had textile and fabric divisions that produced upholstery and vinyl seats in peppy shades. In 1952, US designer Alexander Girard was hired to head Herman Miller's textile division, and he fearlessly introduced fabrics in searing pinks and purples.

Italy, postwar, devoted itself wholeheartedly to its economic reconstruction, embracing modernity – and flamboyant colour – in its new designs. And this optimistic spirit proved contagious, travelling even as far as the US, according to Simon Andrews: 'There were strong links between Italy and America. There was a show in Brooklyn, New York, in 1950 on avant-garde Italian design, around that time American department store Macy's exhibited Gio Ponti's furniture and Olivetti had a shop on New York's Fifth Avenue by 1955.'

MONOCHROME

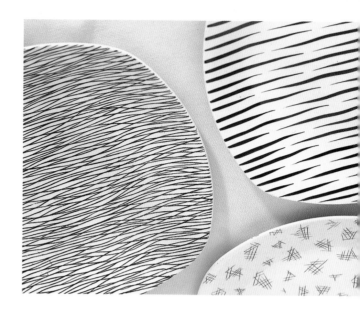

Despite the explosion of colour in the 1950s, a monochrome palette also appealed to designers for its elegance and graphic impact, most obviously the Italian artist and designer Piero Fornasetti. Defying the simplicity of much mid-century design, Fornasetti emblazoned everything from cabinets and umbrella stands to plates with unashamedly decorative Surrealist or Neoclassical imagery. One of his favourite motifs was the enigmatic, alabaster-skinned face of opera singer Lina Cavalieri, pictured on his monochrome series of plates, Themes & Variations. The cabinets Fornasetti decorated (see page 65) were designed by his close collaborator Gio Ponti, whose own Superleggera chair (see page 14) had a very graphic, black frame. Serge Mouille's lamps (see page 114), whose black arms and shades with reflective white interiors allude to light and shadow, were also part of this mini-trend.

Monochrome patterns frequently adorned British ceramics, notably Enid Seeney's iconic 1955 Homemaker china for Ridgway with its silhouetted images of hip, mid-century homeware. And Jessie Tait's Zambesi tableware for Midwinter in 1956 bore a whimsically wiggly, abstract pattern recalling zebra skin; both name and pattern had colonial, tribal, primitivist overtones. Midwinter was run by Roy Midwinter, who, following a sales trip to the US in 1952, returned full of enthusiasm for the ceramics of Russel Wright and Eva Zeisel – another example of the migration of ideas that enriched mid-century design.

French firm Pierre Frey's Altamira wallpaper of 1954, created by Germaine Midy, has a similar vibe to Zambesi, although it was inspired by the discovery of France's Lascaux caves in 1940.

Eero Aarnio's '60s Pastil chair in that non-colour popular in the decade of Op Art and space-age fashion – white.

OPPOSITE, INSET Three 1950s Jessie Tait plates – from left to right, Tonga, Monaco and the zebra-striped Zambesi – for Midwinter. Tait was its chief designer when the company was undergoing a renaissance, thanks to Roy Midwinter. Its ultra-modern, mass-produced ceramics catapulted the Contemporary style into homes everywhere.

An assortment of Russel Wright's influential American Modern tableware in predominantly pastel tones. Via this range, Wright – who also designed glass, cutlery, plastics and furniture – introduced the innovative idea of mix-and-match tableware. In a palette of complementary colours, its pieces harmonized however they were combined.

OPPOSITE Alexander Girard's whimsical Wooden Dolls of 1963 exhibit the cleaner, candy-bright pastels that had come into vogue in the 1950s. Girard's eyes were opened to colour by the vibrantly hued folk art he began collecting in the 1930s.

PASTELS AND MID-TONES

lexander Girard's championing of colour at Herman Miller was paralleled by its widespread use by modernist architects. Le Corbusier's Unité d'Habitation apartment block in Marseille of 1947–52, which had a Mondrian-esque façade – and his habit of painting walls blue, to represent the sky, and ochre, the earth – bucked the modernist convention for all-white architecture and interiors and paved the way for a growing international trend for pastels and mid-tones in 1950s and '60s homes. From 1966, Danish ceramicist Bjørn Wiinblad lived in a house in Copenhagen with a powder blue façade and yellow and lilac interiors.

Eva Zeisel's 1940s Town and Country tableware hinted at the coming vogue for pastels: while mainly in airforce blue and autumnal browns, some pieces were in sharp sherbet yellow. Girard himself created his semi-abstract Wooden Dolls in shades like sugared-almond pink in 1963 for his home in Santa Fe, New Mexico. These are now made by Swiss firm Vitra, which obtained the licence to produce Herman Miller furniture in Europe in 1957. Girard's lust for colour sprang from a passion for South American and Asian folk art.

The Eameses' fiberglass-shell chairs of 1950 – developed with Zenith Plastics for a competition held by MoMA in 1948 called

LEFT AND OPPOSITE
Sludgier pastels and warm mid-tones, such as ochre and mustard, were popular in mid-century homes. One influence on this, perhaps, were avant-garde 1950s textiles, many of which channelled the autumnal, moody, muddy colours favoured by artists such as John Piper and Henry Moore. Incidentally, their own textiles for David Whitehead came in similarly earthy hues like fawn and ochre, spiked with the odd splash of acid yellow or petrol blue.

BELOW The Eameses also championed mid-tones with their fibreglass-seat chairs in both bright and muted pastels.

Low-Cost Furniture Design – were mostly in chalky pastels: lemon yellow, elephant grey, 'seafoam green' and tomato red.

Danish and Finnish metalware and glass frequently came in cool mid-tones. Danish designer Herbert Krenchel's steel Krenit bowls of 1953 were remarkably similar in colour to the aforementioned Eames chairs, while Timo Sarpaneva's 1956 I-glass set of carafe and glasses for Finnish brand Iittala was in sea greens and grapey mauves.

LEFT Jewel-bright, mid-century glass inevitably injected eye-popping colour into fashionable homes. Italian firm Venini on the island of Murano, which made these 1950s light fixtures by Massimo Vignelli, revived ancient techniques such as pezzato. This created crazy-paving-like, multicoloured patterns.

FAR LEFT Danish glassware could be equally vibrant, although it generally came in simpler shapes and solid blocks of colour. These bottle-shaped Carnaby vases made by the Danish firm Holmegaard were designed by Per Lütken, who usually favoured pale colours.

TECHNICOLOUR

While pastels jazzed up 1950s homes, adventurous designers and manufacturers in the US, Italy and Denmark increasingly produced softly contoured, colour-drenched furniture that unwittingly presaged the 1960s Pop movement. At Herman Miller, Alexander Girard noted: 'People had fainting fits if they saw bright, pure colour.' But undeterred, during his tenure there Girard created over 300 textile designs, many in primaries. Some Eames fibreglass-shell chairs for Herman Miller came in intense cornflower blue, while its 1956 Marshmallow sofa by George Nelson comprised rows of Smartie/M&M-like discs in crimson, orange and magenta. The idea behind these separate cushions was that they could be easily upholstered in different colours, unlike a traditional sofa.

RIGHT Upholstery fabrics were highly influential in introducing more colour into interiors. Herman Miller, which added furnishing fabrics to its repertoire in the 1950s – and manufactured the Marshmallow sofa, proof of its uninhibited attitude to colour – was a key player in this regard. And heading up Knoll's textile division was Hungarian-born Eszter Haraszty whose favourite colour combo – very Yves Saint Laurent – was orange and pink. Italian design magazine 'Domus' ran a feature entitled 'The Colours of Eszter Haraszty' picturing a living room in three shades of shocking pink.

BELOW Another arbiter of taste was Jack Lenor Larsen, who designed this outlandishly flamboyant fabric on Pierre Paulin's 1966 Ribbon chair.

OPPOSITE Verner Panton's injection moulded-plastic S chair came in a whole rainbow of colours, including this glossy fire-engine red.

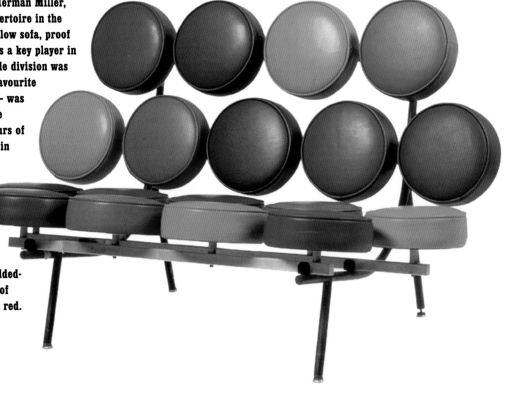

In Denmark, Arne Jacobsen and Verner Panton broke from the Danish tradition of wood-based furniture and pioneered a proto-Pop aesthetic. The stretchy fabrics emphasizing the curves of Jacobsen's Egg and Swan chairs and Panton's 1958 Cone chair came in shades like lipstick red and cobalt blue. By the time he designed his ultra-trippy, rainbow-hued, fabric-lined Visiona II 'total environment' for Bayer at the 1970 Cologne Furniture Fair, Panton was also channelling psychedelia.

In France in the 1960s, Pierre Paulin experimented with swimwear fabric and foam to create his organic yet minimalist Ribbon and Tongue chairs for Artifort – some upholstered in the exuberant fabrics of US designer Jack Lenor Larsen. Olivier Mourgue dreamt up his scarlet Djinn chairs (see page 68), which appeared in the 1968 movie *2001: A Space Odyssey*. Glass designers let rip with colour, too. Murano in Italy enjoyed a renaissance, with venerable but visionary companies like Venini making unapologetically polychrome pieces by such avant-garde names as Carlo Scarpa and Fulvio Bianconi.

OPPOSITE Lucienne Day's iconic Calyx fabric. Like her husband Robin, Lucienne believed design should be democratic and accessible, and found it gratifying that anyone who couldn't afford a modernist painting could own a pair of abstract-patterned curtains.

RIGHT An array of 1950s fabrics, including Stig Lindberg's design Pottery of 1947 used to cover a cushion, grace a living room.

FAR RIGHT A semi-abstract 1954 fabric depicting book spines created by the Czech-born, London-based textile designer Jacqueline Groag for Liberty.

PATTERN, IMAGERY AND THEMES

Along with the resurgence of colour in the 1950s came a passion for pattern. After the deprivations of the war, a more inclusive, relaxed attitude to design – combined with a yearning for frivolity and humour – stoked up an appetite for ornamentation and surface pattern. Figurative imagery was rife, too, thanks partly to a modish, postwar affection for whimsical, mood-lightening folk culture, including a fad for hot-air balloon motifs – which bubbled up the front of one Piero Fornasetti screen – and ornate, Victorian fairground-inspired images. Textiles, ceramics and glass were also influenced by the loose, gestural, splashy aesthetic of 1950s abstract art. Moreover, a fascination with science – from microbiology and chemistry to space exploration – left its mark on architecture and design.

This hunger for the decorative, particularly among a younger, increasingly affluent and independent generation rebelling against aesthetic conservatism, was boosted by greater prosperity. This was greatly fuelled by the Marshall Plan, which, between 1948 and 1951, saw the US give $13bn to European countries that were members of the Organization for European Economic Cooperation to help them rebuild their economies. By 1952, every participating state's output was over 35 per cent higher than in 1938.

ABSTRACT

Many found postwar abstract art 'difficult', but abstract patterns in the home – and fashion – became increasingly common as the 1950s progressed. These manifested themselves both in high-end and populist design, colonizing Formica-topped tables, curtains and linoleum. That these were more easily accepted than abstract art wasn't perhaps surprising. After all, abstract textiles and ceramics had existed for centuries and so were familiar.

Meanwhile, more bohemian homes, like the Eameses' – which jumbled richly patterned Navaho and Mexican crafts with abstract art by Hans Hofmann – infused the pared-down, abstract aesthetic of 1950s modernism with a cosier, folksier feel.

Motifs from 1950s abstract or semi-abstract art crossed over into the domestic sphere thanks partly to the phenomenon of

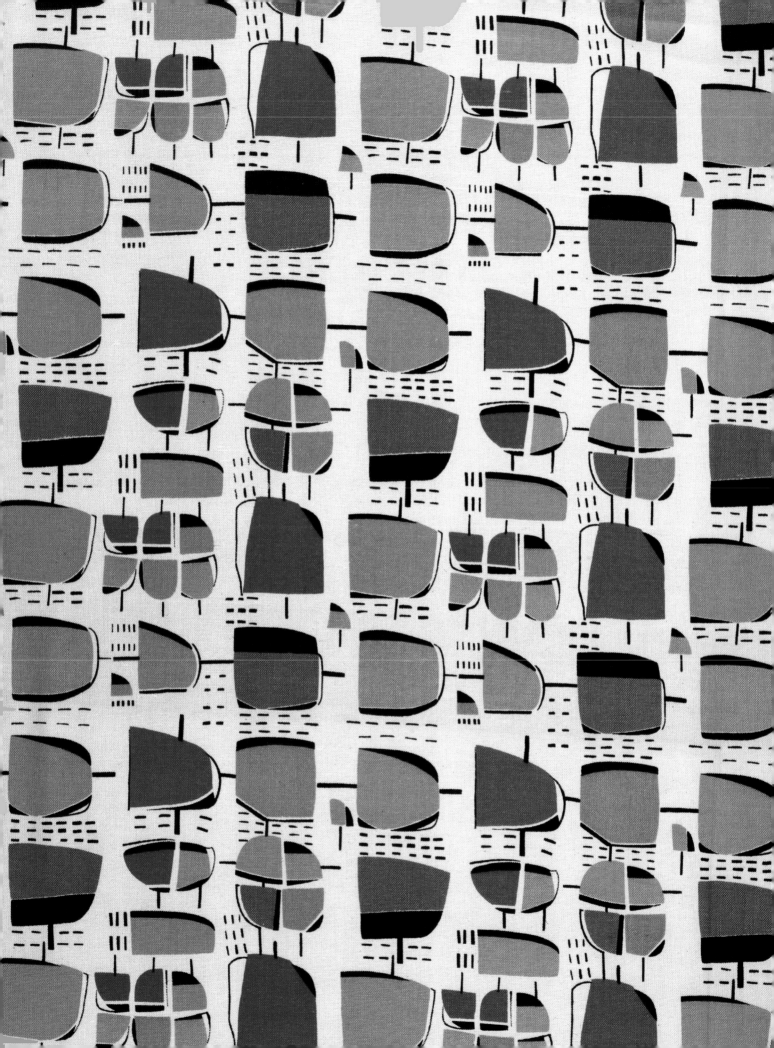

OPPOSITE British artist and designer Harold Cohen's Vineyard furnishing fabric for Heal's. Inspired by Jackson Pollock, this was less straightforwardly decorative and more challenging than many abstract textiles.

RIGHT Textile designer Barbara Brown also designed tableware, such as this 1964 Focus coffee pot for Midwinter, which has Op Art overtones.

artist-designed textiles created by the likes of John Piper and Henry Moore for British textiles manufacturer David Whitehead. And avant-garde, London-based fabric makers Zika and Lida Ascher appreciated the design potential of abstract patterns, commissioning artists including Moore, Barbara Hepworth, Paul Nash and abstract painter Nicholas de Staël to create their 'artists' scarves' from 1946 to 1955.

By the late 1950s, the more radically non-representational art movements of Abstract Expressionism in the US and Tachisme in France (from the French word *tache*, meaning 'stain') also influenced design. This was glaringly evident, for example, in Harold Cohen's 1959 fabric Vineyard for Heal's – a cross between a Rorschach blot and Jackson Pollock painting. Some designs, including by Lucienne Day, were printed on new synthetic fabric acetate rayon, which accentuated their modernity.

Mid-century glass and metalware were often textured, creating surfaces that formed abstract patterns. Tapio Wirkkala, who trained as a sculptor, designed his Ultima Thule glassware range for Iittala. Reminiscent of chunks of ice, this was inspired by visits to the rugged landscapes of Lapland. In Britain, silversmith Gerald Benney was one of the first pioneers of abstract, textured surfaces

on metal, as seen for example on his silver goblet of 1957 and highly successful 1960s stainless steel cutlery.

By the 1960s, influenced in part by Op Art's geometric images and the paintings of Victor Vasarely, abstract-patterned fabrics became brazenly large scale. There were Barbara Brown's 1960s and '70s fabrics with outsized, abstract motifs for Heal's, Verner Panton's rugs and textiles for Swiss firm Mira-X and Maija Isola's textiles for Finland's Marimekko, including her 1964 design Kaivo, inspired by her dropping a bucket into a well and seeing the water rippling dramatically.

LEFT AND BELOW LEFT **Midwinter didn't confine itself to abstract patterns. Jessie Tait's autumn-themed Falling Leaves plate and Terence Conran's Salad Ware dish, designed for Midwinter in 1955, featured stylized figurative motifs.**

BOTTOM LEFT **Swedish ceramicist Stig Lindberg created this doubly figurative bowl – it was shaped like a leaf and bore a leaf pattern – in the 1950s.**

OPPOSITE **The preponderance of abstract motifs in avant-garde art and design didn't deter designers from using figurative imagery. Josef Frank detested the abstract aesthetic of much modernist architecture, so it was logical that he created irreverently figurative, flagrantly decorative textiles, such as his 1943 Hawaii fabric.**

FIGURATIVE

In the 1950s, figurative imagery provided an easier entry point into the mid-century aesthetic than abstract patterns. Although often highly stylized and semi-abstract, figurative imagery was still reassuringly recognizable. People also familiarized themselves with this via the contemporary illustrations and graphics of the likes of Tom Eckersley, Eric Ravilious and Abram Games, who created the Festival of Britain's official emblem, which fused Britannia's profile, compass points and a necklace-like garland of fluttering bunting in jaunty red, white and blue.

An early sign of a return to figurative imagery as an alternative to abstraction could be found in the 1940s textiles of Austrian architect and designer Josef Frank, who moved to Stockholm in 1933. In the 1920s, he had rebelled against modernism, finding it monotonous and po-faced; he even espoused unpretentious kitsch as an antidote to it. His busy, exuberant, almost proto-psychedelic fabrics for Swedish firm Svenskt Tenn – for example, Hawaii, which bursts with paradisiacal fruit and flowers – were the antithesis of modernist 'good' taste.

While figurative motifs appealed to many because of their familiarity, Piero Fornasetti's were often Surrealist and arrestingly unfamiliar. Yet they helped popularize figurative imagery, partly because they were also richly decorative. So, too, did Pablo Picasso's sculptural jugs for French pottery Vallauris, which featured human figures and mythological creatures, and artist Jean Cocteau's plates with human faces.

Meanwhile, Bjørn Wiinblad's ceramics for Rosenthal and Danish pottery Nymølle brimmed with ultra-stylized, round-faced figures like ballerinas and courting couples, often framed by twirling vines and floral wreaths. Their mannered, faux-naif style – like that of his contemporary, the British illustrator and cartoonist Rowland Emett – gave them a droll, whimsical feel.

More straightforward was figurative imagery drawn from nature. Ceramicist Stig Lindberg, chief designer at Swedish pottery Gustavsberg, hand-painted platters with leaves, while some of his bowls were shaped like curling leaves and painted with veins, so figurative both in their form and pattern.

The most accessible figurative imagery of the 1950s domesticated nature, depicting it as food, appropriately on designs for the kitchen. Terence Conran's 1955 Salad Ware pattern for Midwinter featured dancing onions and tomatoes. Swedish ceramicist Marianne Westman's Picknick tableware of 1956 pictured pea pods and herbs. And a kitchen wallpaper called Slices, produced in 1953 by US company Herndon Papers, marshalled cross-sections of apples and peppers into neat rows.

RIGHT AND ABOVE **Piero Fornasetti's Architettura sideboard-cum-desk of 1951 features trompe l'oeil images of various architectural perspectives lithographically printed on a cabinet designed by Gio Ponti. Famous for his figurative imagery, Fornasetti was inspired throughout his life by Neoclassical iconography, as evidenced, too, by his Pompeiana screen designed some years later.**

OPPOSITE **Fornasetti's conceit is echoed by this cabinet designed by British husband-and-wife team Robert and Dorothy Heritage in 1954. Fronted with a townscape drawn in a graphic, modern style, it was produced by London-based manufacturer GW Evans.**

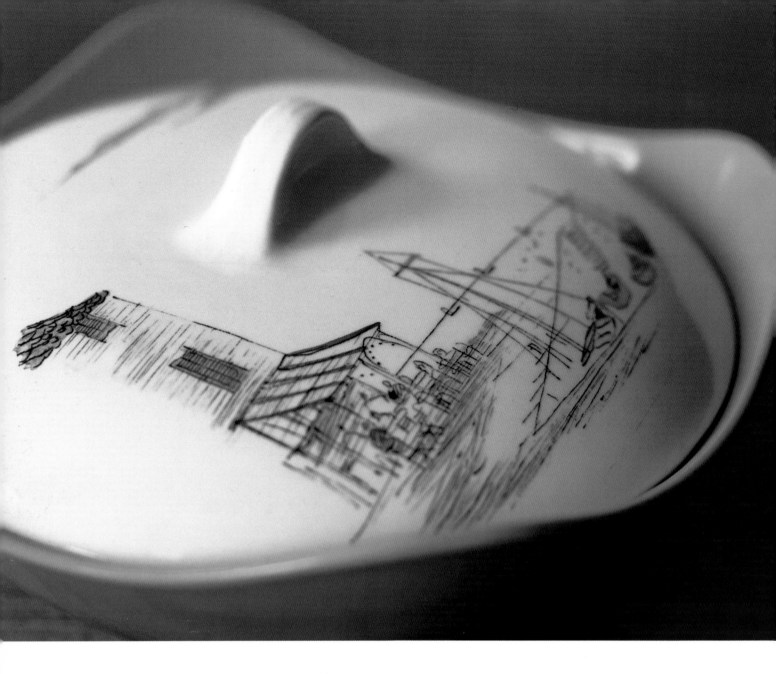

WHIMSICAL

The cartoony nature of much figurative imagery often tipped it over into the realm of whimsy. Its unapologetically cute, childlike look – Wiinblad's figures, for example, were doll-like – also made it whimsical. Arguably, whimsical postwar imagery, which had its roots in a late 1940s feel-good trend for folk art, including Victorian fairground imagery, was symptomatic of a desire to blot out horrific memories of the war. The same could be said for the abundance of cutesy animal imagery – and chairs named after animals: Eero Saarinen's Grasshopper Chair and Ottoman of 1946, Ernest Race's Antelope and Springbok and Arne Jacobsen's Ant and Swan. 'There was a childlike engagement with nature in reaction to wartime destruction,' believes Simon Andrews. 'These names are revealing. They were all about softening the hard edges of modernist furniture.' Some mid-century furniture, such as Ernst Moeckl's 1960s Kangaroo chair with bent knee-like legs for East German company Horn, was overtly whimsical.

Kooky, cartoony imagery graced ceramics from Stig Lindberg's plate featuring a faux-naif design of clothes on washing lines from his 1940s Faience range to Piero Fornasetti's 1950s salad bowls picturing anthropomorphic fruit and vegetables with human faces.

And the anything-goes attitude of many Murano glass companies in the 1950s and '60s yielded a slew of animal-shaped pieces that some considered endearing, others kitsch knick-knacks. In 1961, Vetreria Vistosi made designer Alessandro Pianon's almost comical figurines of chicks with spindly wire legs. Other Murano critters took the form of horses, swans, fishes and cockerels.

OPPOSITE Architect and designer Hugh Casson – who was the Festival of Britain's architecture director – created this Cannes tureen in fashionable, sugared-almond pastels for Midwinter in 1954.

LEFT A collection of Bjørn Wiinblad's typically whimsical, doll-like ceramic figurines; their attire reflects the 1950s revival of Victorian and Edwardian imagery and folk art.

ABOVE A fabric called Gala designed by Jacqueline Groag in the late 1940s for Manchester-based firm FW Grafton & Co.

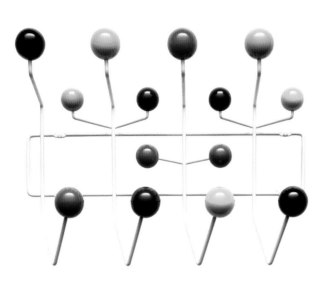

ABOVE The Eameses' 1953 Hang-It-All coatrack – conceived to encourage children to hang up their stuff – reflected the trend for molecular motifs, mainly kicked off by Ernest Race's 1951 Antelope chair with its ball-shaped feet.

RIGHT Olivier Mourgue's Djinn chair – an iconic example of space age-chic design – appeared in Stanley Kubrick's film '2001: A Space Odyssey'.

BELOW Per Lütken's 1956 Provence bowl for Holmegaard anticipated the '60s vogue for Perspex design.

SCIENCE

Science postwar was viewed with ambivalence: it either symbolized a better future or the Cold War and menace of nuclear weapons. Yet nothing could suppress people's enthusiasm for new discoveries in chemistry, microbiology and space exploration, not to mention science fiction. Space exploration skyrocketed in the 1950s – a decade also dubbed the Atomic Age – with Russia launching its Sputnik I satellite in 1957 and the US its Explorer I satellite in 1958. 'Science was a major inspiration,' says Corinne Julius. 'People believed that science, education, design and architecture could improve their lives.'

In design, this spawned forms and patterns based on crystalline, molecular and atomic structures – fashioned into clocks by George Nelson – rocket or flying saucer-shaped lighting and furniture created from futuristic plastics, Perspex and synthetic fibres.

Scientific imagery loomed large in major 1950s exhibitions. The Festival of Britain's spaceship-like Dome of Discovery celebrated achievements in medicine and space exploration. The Brussels World's Fair of 1958 was

Stephen Foster's early 1970s Aphelion TV.
Its shape suggests an astronaut's helmet, its
name an interest in space travel – 'aphelion'
is the point in the orbit of a planet or comet
that's furthest from the sun.

dominated by The Atomium, a gigantic model of a molecular structure.

Design based on scientific imagery was encouraged by UK initiative The Festival Pattern Group, founded in 1949. Designers were provided with X-ray crystallography diagrams by a Cambridge University scientist, then asked to create abstract patterns derived from crystal structures. The resulting unexpectedly decorative wares, which adorned parts of the Festival of Britain, included two wallpapers made by British firm John Line whose names – Insulin and Boric Acid – flaunted their scientific origins.

OPPOSITE Eero Aarnio's Ball chair of 1963 crossed space-age chic with the extreme, geometric simplicity of much 1960s design. Aarnio described it as a private 'room within a room' for the sitter.

ABOVE If Aarnio's Ball chair isolated the sitter, his transparent soap bubble-shaped 1968 Bubble chair was more social.

LEFT Erwine and Estelle Laverne's radically avant-garde acrylic Lily chair of 1957 – part of their Invisible Group of see-through furniture – anticipated the transparent plastic design vogue by a decade.

MID-CENTURY
COLLECTIBLES

The mid-century aesthetic pervaded every field of design, from furniture to ceramics, glass to lighting. Avant-garde architects sought to furnish their buildings with equally modern designs, and forward-thinking manufacturers and designers satisfied this demand, while consumers lapped up their ideas. Postwar construction of social housing, smaller homes and more informal lifestyles also fuelled the trend for practical yet stylish design.

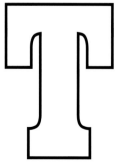

LEFT Charles and Ray Eames's classic armchairs, on the left, and LCM and LCW chairs, on the right, form a harmonious whole in this room. 'Time Magazine' hailed their moulded plywood chairs, which have slightly flexible backrests, the Best Design of the 20th Century.

ABOVE Hans Wegner's 1960 Ox chair stands on the left, his 1949 CH25 chairs (for Carl Hansen) to the right. The Ox was his favourite chair, gracing his living room until he died. The CH25's seat and backrest are made from hand-woven paper cord.

CHAIRS

The protagonist of mid-century design is undoubtedly the chair. Of course, chairs are one of our most necessary pieces of furniture. But more to the point, it was when creating chairs that mid-century designers were at their most inventive. Tellingly, pioneering chair designers the Eameses are much better known than, for example, Enid Seeney, the creator of the hugely popular 1950s Homemaker crockery.

DINING AND STACKING CHAIRS

There were two main, distinct types of mid-century chair: the capacious lounge or armchair, which reflected the new vogue for lounging and sprawling and was symptomatic of an increasingly laid-back, postwar lifestyle, and the more practical dining or stacking chair.

Epitomizing the latter is Arne Jacobsen's stackable, teak ply Series 7: No 3107 chair of 1955, a development of his 1952 Ant chair, whose use of lamination emulated the way the Eameses had successfully bent wood in several directions on one piece of furniture. Some say the stripped-down 3107 was commissioned by Danish manufacturer Fritz Hansen to accompany its dining tables;

OPPOSITE Several Eames Plastic Side chairs of 1950 (which originally featured fibreglass seats) encircle a dining table. True to mid-century's democratic spirit, these were developed for MoMA's 1948 Low-Cost Furniture Design competition in collaboration with Zenith Plastics. They were the world's first industrially produced plastic chairs.

LEFT Dutch designer Cees Braakman created his SM05 chair in fashionably transparent steel wire in 1958 for the Utrecht-based, avant-garde furniture manufacturer Pastoe. Braakman was head of Pastoe's design team from 1945 to 1978.

ABOVE Stackable and lightweight, Arne Jacobsen's No 3107 chair satisfies all the criteria of mid-century design. Its manufacturer Fritz Hansen has sold five million of these chairs since they were launched in 1955.

LEFT Joe Colombo's 1965 stackable Universale chair, made by Italian company Kartell, is also height-adjustable: its legs can be unscrewed and replaced with longer ones to make it taller.

BELOW Eero Saarinen's background as a sculptor influenced the form of his Tulip chair, produced by Knoll from 1956. He made clay models of it, which he obsessively modified. Real chairs were later tested by his friends at his home in Michigan.

OPPOSITE In 1972, Robin Day designed another polypropylene chair – the Polo, intended for indoor and outdoor use. In 2000, Day granted UK manufacturer Loft the licence to reproduce his (literally and metaphorically) groovy Polo.

others that Jacobsen designed it for his building, Rødovre Town Hall, in Denmark. Whatever its precise origin, the 3107 is still Fritz Hansen's best-selling chair and one of the most copied, legendary chairs of all time. Popular mythology holds that Christine Keeler bestrode the 3107 naked in Lewis Morley's famous photograph of her, but it was in fact a copy. Unwittingly, Morley's saucy snap reinforced the original design's bracingly modern image and massively boosted its sales. The 3107 also won the Grand Prix at the Milan Triennale in 1957, which helped cement Jacobsen's international reputation.

Chairs such as the 3107 held huge appeal in the 1950s, for example in the US, where thousands of GIs and their families craved simple, practical, easily portable, space-saving furniture that was suited to smaller, postwar homes. In 1950, Charles and Ray Eames, too, created a mass-produced, stackable, moulded plastic side chair with lightweight aluminium legs. And, given that they advocated mass-production because it allowed more people to buy good design, their stacking – and dining – chairs had democratic connotations.

British designer Robin Day also fervently believed in the democratic principle of good design available to all. He achieved this goal with his 1963 low-cost, ultra-durable, stacking polypropylene

OPPOSITE, INSET Ernest Race's early BA3 cast-aluminium chair demonstrates his innovative use of materials. Its manufacture deployed technology originally pioneered for aircraft and car manufacturers. It was unveiled at the 1946 Victoria and Albert Museum exhibition Britain Can Make It, which showcased cutting-edge design.

OPPOSITE Race's Antelope chair was designed for the outdoor terraces of the newly built Royal Festival Hall during the Festival of Britain in 1951. Its innovative, economical frame typified the so-called 'Contemporary' style of the 1950s, which saw countless products, from magazine racks to plant holders, sport splayed legs and molecular ball feet.

RIGHT Hans Wegner held traditional joinery in high esteem yet reinterpreted it in a modern way. His Wishbone (or CH24) chair, on the right, was made by Copenhagen manufacturer Carl Hansen. Its name derives from its comfortable, Y-shaped backrest.

BELOW The Eameses' sleek and curvaceous Plywood Group DCM chairs.

chair for Hille: this bestselling, institutional yet super-Pop design is still in production and has graced schools, hospitals and canteens the world over.

Even the more formal dining chair was relatively pared down and skeletal, and so perfectly suited the new style of modern, transparent, uncluttered interior. However, some tapped into tradition, too. Danish designer Hans Wegner's 1949 skeletal-sounding Wishbone chair for Carl Hansen was both finely crafted from wood and inspired by the past – specifically, by a portrait of Danish merchants sitting on Ming Dynasty chairs.

This light, bright living room is suitably uncluttered, despite its array of mid-century-style furniture and authentic mid-century pieces, including the Eameses' LCW chair.

OPPOSITE Alvar Aalto's ergonomic Paimio chair, designed for Finland's Paimio Sanatorium for tuberculosis patients. It was exhibited at the 1939 New York World's Fair, bringing it to a wider US audience.

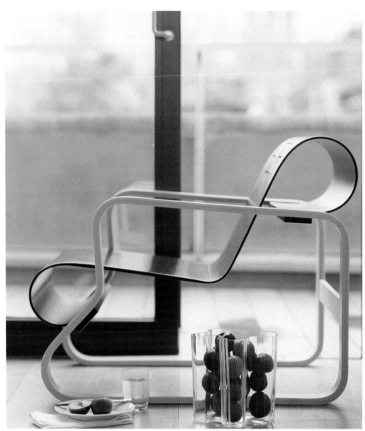

LOUNGE CHAIRS AND ARMCHAIRS

Playing a more prominent role than the stacking or dining chair was the scene-stealing lounge or armchair. Its newly exalted status was partly assured by avant-garde architects who prized its sculptural qualities, a fetish amply catered to by many designers who had strong links with sculpture. Eero Saarinen, for example, trained as a sculptor, while Isamu Noguchi, who was brought up in the US and Japan, studied under sculptor Constantin Brancusi. 'The chair is as much a sculpture as an object of utility,' declared George Nelson. 'The once-humble chair has emerged as a thoroughly glamorous object.'

In the US, there was a close, symbiotic relationship between such manufacturers as Herman Miller and Knoll and architects like Richard Neutra, who often picked

these firms' furniture to complement their radically open-plan interiors. Neutra was one of several prominent architects commissioned to design the postwar, experimental, residential Case Study Houses, sponsored by *Arts & Architecture* magazine and built mainly in Los Angeles. In open-plan homes such as these, it was important that the new chairs made an impact from all angles – rather like sculptures in a gallery. A growing trend for built-in furniture also made these chairs more conspicuous.

Although influenced by sculpture, these chairs weren't put on a pedestal but were

OPPOSITE ABOVE LEFT Børge Mogensen's oak and leather Hunting chair was designed in 1950 for the Copenhagen Cabinetmakers' Guild autumn exhibition, whose theme was 'The Hunting lodge'. It resembles Mogensen's Spanish chair of 1958.

OPPOSITE ABOVE RIGHT Danish designer Jørgen Høvelskov's idiosyncratic 1968 Harp chair was inspired by a Viking ship's bow. In true mid-century style, its invitingly reclining backrest encouraged laid-back lounging.

OPPOSITE BELOW Danish designer Poul Kjaerholm's mid-1950s stripped-down yet comfortable PK22 chair scooped the Grand Prix at the 1957 Milan Triennale. Originally made by E Kold Christensen, it is now manufactured by Fritz Hansen.

RIGHT Arne Jacobsen's voluptously curvaceous 1958 Egg chair, designed for the SAS Royal Hotel in Copenhagen.

BELOW Nanna Ditzel's 1957 rattan hanging chair epitomizes the organic, cocooning character of much mid-century seating.

designed to be indulgently comfortable. In stark contrast to early modernist chairs, with their right angles and low backrests seemingly calculated to encourage earnest conversation, their mid-century counterparts were sensual, with soft edges and wide, fanning, enveloping, sometimes cocooning backrests – obvious examples being the Womb, Egg and Ball chairs.

In postwar Europe, exciting developments in chair design were partly precipitated by a search for new materials to compensate for a shortage of timber and metals, which had been reserved for the war effort. The discovery

ABOVE **Harry Bertoia's 1952 Bird chair for Knoll is the high-backed version of his Diamond chair (on the left in the right-hand picture). Bertoia was also a sculptor and, arguably, his wire-rod chairs were inspired by Naum Gabo's sculptures incorporating tautly stretched string.**

RIGHT **George Nelson's 1955 Coconut chair, on the far right, is similarly capacious. Nelson took the trend for furniture with organic-sounding names further with edible-sounding monickers for this chair shaped like a coconut slice (for Herman Miller) and his Marshmallow sofa.**

in Italy of foam rubber and in Denmark of foam padding made from polystyrene beads steamed to form almost any shape facilitated the creation of extravagantly organic chairs. Taking their cue initially from the Eameses' free-form La Chaise, these also fulfilled Florence Knoll's wish that chairs should be liberatingly casual, allowing the sitter to assume any number of positions.

ABOVE **Robin Day's Reclining chair of 1952 for British manufacturer Hille, on the left, has slender legs to ensure that it is unimposing. 'What one needs in today's small rooms is to see over and under one's furniture,' he told a journalist in 1955. The chair to the right has similarly slimline, sled-like legs.**

LEFT **Charles and Ray Eames's 1956 Lounge Chair and Ottoman has become associated with art directors, but Ray once remarked to Charles that it looked 'comfortable and un-designy'.**

RIGHT **Eero Saarinen's Tulip chairs were designed to complement his Tulip table – the whole ensemble was also known as his 'pedestal collection'. Appropriately, in the 1960s, these space age-chic chairs graced Star Trek's Starship Enterprise.**

BELOW **The Tulip chairs' manufacturer Knoll also made Florence Knoll's sofa. Knoll's co-founder Hans Knoll was born in Germany and emigrated to New York in 1937 where he co-founded Knoll, inspired by the realization that architects needed well-designed, contemporary furniture for their buildings.**

SOFAS

In contrast to the show-stopping sofas and daybeds made of sumptuous materials created by such Art Deco designers as Jacques-Emile Ruhlmann, mid-century sofas were mostly boxy, unassuming and quietly elegant, like those, say, of Ernest Race and George Nelson. One reason for this was that, in the 1950s, sofas were often associated with the traditional three-piece suite, which – in smaller mid-century homes, where space was at a premium and clutter discouraged – looked cumbersome, indeed superannuated. And sofas took a back seat to the statement-making lounge chair.

OPPOSITE ABOVE **Olivier Mourgue's ultra-pop Djinn chaise longue.** Manufactured by Airborne in France in 1964, it was part of a range that also included a chair and sofa. The name 'Djinn' refers to a shape-shifting Islamic spirit, while the chaise's low-level design reflects the 1960s craze for informal, bohemian seating.

OPPOSITE BELOW **Børge Mogensen,** whose designs exemplified mid-century's softer take on modernism, created his squashy 2213 sofa in 1962. His 1950s Spanish chairs can be seen in the foreground.

ABOVE **Austrian designer Josef Hoffmann** created these Kubus sofas in 1910, but in terms of sheer comfort, they presaged mid-century's love of commodious furniture.

RIGHT **The Eameses' ground-breaking La Chaise seat of 1948.**

RIGHT While the mid-century lounge chair was often attention-grabbing for being curvaceous and in an arresting shape, sofas and daybeds from the same period – like this one – were relatively understated.

OPPOSITE This daybed with an oak and steel frame painted black, called Antony, was designed by Jean Prouvé in 1954 for a student hall of residence in Antony, near Paris. It's in fact dual-functional: attached to it is a shelf that swivels.

BELOW Frankfurt-born architect and designer Ferdinand Kramer's simple but luxe Theban daybed of 1925 – now made by German manufacturer e15 – anticipated the mid-century taste for plain shapes and natural materials, in this case an oak frame teamed with a woven-leather top.

There were exceptions, of course. George Nelson's Marshmallow sofa (see page 54) hogged both space and the limelight for being seductively colourful and structurally inventive: its fragmented upholstery, whittled down to rows of cushions, arguably anticipated the trend for deconstruction in design. There was nothing reticent either about the pumped-up curves of the 1950 Serpentine sofa by German-born designer Vladimir Kagan (see page 38).

Meanwhile, Florence Knoll's Lounge sofa (see page 41) straddled geometric simplicity and luxury, its plump upholstery, divided into neat cubes, even recalling a chocolate bar.

STOOLS AND BENCHES

OPPOSITE **Ray Eames designed this walnut stool in 1960 for the lobby of the Time & Life building in New York. It's one of a set of different stools, each with a differently shaped, totem-like base, manufactured by Herman Miller. It illustrates the Eameses' eclectic taste, which was influenced by non-Western cultures and sometimes strayed from their predominantly technology-orientated aesthetic.**

ABOVE **Sori Yanagi's Butterfly stool more than makes up for its diminutive scale with its quirky structure. Although it's symmetrical, its two bent-ply elements look sensually organic.**

ABOVE RIGHT **Aalto's best-selling Stool 60 is remarkably robust. Legend has it that he hurled the prototype to the ground to test its sturdiness, exclaiming prophetically, 'We'll make thousands of these one day!'**

RIGHT **Saarinen's Tulip stool – a mini version of the table and chairs from the same family.**

The apparently humble stool was a huge hit in fashionable mid-century homes. This wasn't surprising, since it satisfied so many needs of the time: it was practical, portable, unimposing and space-saving (particularly if stackable). With Alvar Aalto's classic stacking Stool 60 of 1933, created for his building the Viipuri Library in Finland, the stool entered the mid-century design lexicon once and for all. In fact, some of the most iconic mid-century pieces are stools, another being Achille and Pier Giacomo Castiglioni's Mezzadro seat (see page 15). A similarly emblematic, mid-century piece is Japanese industrial designer Sori Yanagi's Butterfly stool of 1956, its unorthodox structure – two bent-ply seat

shells flicking upwards at their ends and joined by a metal rod – inevitably making it memorable. Two years earlier, Yanagi had designed his stackable plastic Elephant stool for both indoor and outdoor use.

Arguably, stools also appealed for being dual-functional – they could double up as dinky side tables. Indeed, many designers addressed the growing demand for multifunctional, space-saving furniture that helped interiors look more streamlined with a whole host of ideas, which included versatile storage units.

Lateral thinking led some designers to treat the neutral nature of a plain bench as a potentially multifunctional surface, too, as George Nelson did with his Platform bench of 1946, conceived to be used as seating, a coffee table or for displaying plants.

TOP **Finnish designer Antti Nurmesniemi's laminated birch Sauna stool of 1952.**

ABOVE **Ercol's understated elm and beech Loveseat was designed in 1956 by Lucian Ercolani, the founder of British manufacturer Ercol who made it. It was inspired by the Windsor chair – as was Hans Wegner's 1947 Peacock chair – and traditional English settle, and designed as a dining bench or two-seater bench.**

ABOVE A mini mid-century trend for multifunctional benches was kick-started by George Nelson's unadorned Platform bench for Herman Miller. The company's ad for it trumpeted: 'This versatile platform bench by George Nelson can serve as a table, a base for a storage cabinet, a bench or plant rest. Truly a multi-purpose piece.'

RIGHT Similarly plain and multifunctional was Robin Day's bench-cum-coffee table – part of his 1950s Interplan range for Hille. Rosamind and Leslie Julius, who ran this uncompromisingly modernist furniture company, began commissioning pieces by Day in 1950.

BEDS

Beds tended to be less showy and more functional than most other types of mid-century furniture. Bedrooms in mid-century homes were often smaller than the more spacious, open-plan living-cum-dining room, and perhaps homeowners preferred to reserve their swankier pieces for the latter.

George Nelson's 1955 Thin Edge bed for Herman Miller is the archetypal mid-century bed. Like his Platform bench, it's extremely understated. Made of wafer-thin laminated wood, its base rests on six slender steel legs, while the headboard is sometimes faced with subtly decorative cane. Zinc-plated perforated steel inserts in the base allow the mattress to breathe.

OPPOSITE The furniture in mid-century bedrooms, including beds themselves, were generally less flamboyant than pieces found in larger, open-plan living rooms, as this bedroom in a 1950s house in Palm Springs – with its ultra-simple bed, headboard and neutral décor – illustrates.

The bed here, in the 1957 Palm Springs home of mid-century dealer Andrew Weaving, is similarly understated. The headboard, which doubles as wall-hung built-in storage, illustrates the mid-century trend for multifunctional furniture.

Mid-century tables were often relatively simple. This round table and the console on the right are by UK designer Robert Heritage for Archie Shine.

RIGHT The teak and stainless steel chairs and dining table are by British designers John and Sylvia Reid for Stag Furniture.

TABLES

At their most adventurous, mid-century tables mirrored experiments carried out in other areas of design. Influenced by moulded plywood technology and a passion for aerial acrobatics, Italian architect and designer Carlo Mollino created his eccentric 1949 Arabesque table, comprising wackily sinuous bent-ply legs with biomorphic shapes cut out of them and two asymmetric glass tops. Mollino's maverick approach typified the devil-may-care individualism of postwar Italian design.

In Britain, the US and Denmark, designers and manufacturers tended to make elegantly simple tables in teak (highly favoured in Denmark) or ultra-fashionable, yellowy red, syrup-hued rosewood. Danish designers Peter Hvidt and Orla Mølgaard-Nielsen produced sober-looking teak dining tables and British firm Archie Shine rosewood dining tables with clean-lined aluminium legs.

ABOVE The Eameses' ETR Elliptical coffee table, whose relaxed informality is emphasized by its low level and surfboard-inspired top.

LEFT Neil Morris's Clouds table of 1947 has an overtly organic, cloud-shaped top. It came in a variety of woods from Honduras mahogany to bird's eye maple. It was made by British company H Morris & Co, which was founded by Neil's father Harris. Neil Morris also created a bedroom suite as a wedding present for Princess Elizabeth and Prince Philip.

COFFEE TABLES

Low-level, casual, lightweight and reasonably portable, the coffee table greatly appealed to mid-century fans with increasingly informal lifestyles. Still, many avant-garde designers applied the same experimental approach to this seemingly inconsequential item as they did to more formal furniture. Visually, Charles and Ray Eames's 1951 ETR Elliptical coffee table belonged to a family of similar-looking products; its criss-crossing metal legs cross-referenced the DAR chair's Eiffel Tower legs. In keeping with its informal vibe, the table was inspired by California's nascent surfing craze, hence its surfboard-like plywood top.

Some furniture collections deliberately incorporated coffee tables that were scaled-down versions of the dining table. Warren Platner's 1725 wire-rod furniture series included a glass-topped coffee table, while Eero Saarinen's marble-topped Tulip dining

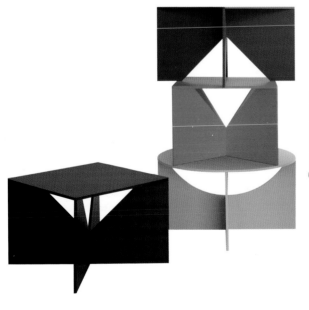

ABOVE British-born TH Robsjohn-Gibbings, who studied architecture at London University and later worked in the US as an interior designer and furniture designer for the manufacturer Widdicomb, created his Aalto-esque Mesa table in the 1950s.

LEFT Ferdinand Kramer's square Calvert and circular Charlotte coffee tables of 1951 – manufactured today by German company e15 – were part of his Knock-Down furniture series. Made of oak or walnut veneer or finished with coloured lacquer, they were ahead of their time for being collapsible and space-saving.

RIGHT As with this table from Warren Platner's 1725 furniture series, mid-century coffee tables were often part of a bigger family of furniture.

OPPOSITE Isamu Noguchi's coffee table was a later version of a rosewood and glass table he designed in 1939 for Anson Goodyear, president of MoMA. Herman Miller's design team was so impressed by it that they asked Noguchi to design a similar one.

BELOW This table made by British manufacturer Arkana emulated Eero Saarinen's iconic Tulip side table.

table was cloned into a coordinating coffee table and side table. The message this sent was anti-hierarchical: the informal coffee table was no less important than grander dining tables.

America's 'studio furniture' movement produced ruggedly organic, often handcrafted, wood pieces, including coffee tables, all close in spirit to 19th-century Arts and Crafts furniture. A key exponent, Japanese-American woodworker George Nakashima made raw-edged, hand-carved coffee tables using timber cherry-picked for its decorative knots and grain (see page 20). Phillip Lloyd Powell created a walnut bench incorporating a coffee table, and TH Robsjohn-Gibbings designed walnut coffee tables for US furniture firm Widdicomb in simple, accessible shapes.

The most iconic mid-century coffee table is Isamu Noguchi's biomorphic table of 1944 for Herman Miller. Supporting its glass top are two wood elements, whose organic forms echo those of his Arp-inspired, interlocking abstract sculptures.

The multi-talented designer George Nelson turned his hand to all kinds of furniture, including simple, boxy chests of drawers, such as this one in Andrew Weaving's London home. The piece is typically mid-century for standing on spindly 'hairpin legs', creating a style that's top-heavy yet elegant.

CABINETRY AND STORAGE

Storage played a pivotal role in the development of mid-century design, thanks in particular to one of its key innovators, George Nelson. Nelson studied architecture at Yale University, then wrote articles in the journal *Pencil Points* about such modernist titans as Mies van der Rohe, Le Corbusier and Gio Ponti, which introduced European modernism to many American readers. In 1945, he and designer Henry Wright co-wrote *Tomorrow's House*, which explored ideas about open-plan living and included Nelson's influential, space-saving concept, the Storagewall. This proposed recessed, built-in shelving in the unused space within wall cavities in houses, a brainwave that prompted DJ De Pree, president of Herman Miller, to manufacture it – and appoint Nelson as the firm's design director in 1946. Nelson in turn hired and nurtured such talents as the Eameses, Bertoia and Noguchi, thereby directly influencing design history. Under his supervision, the Eameses created their fashionably multifunctional ESU shelving unit.

LEFT **Austrian architect Egon Riis's Penguin Donkey bookcase was made by the Isokon Furniture Company, and held about 80 Penguin paperbacks. Only about 100 bookcases were manufactured, and production ceased during the war due to a shortage of materials.**

ABOVE **Alvar Aalto's Tea Trolley – inspired structurally by the Paimio chair and launched at the Paris World's Fair in 1937 – doubles as storage with its cane basket. It's made by Artek, the company Aalto co-founded in Helsinki in 1935.**

Although mid-century hipsters reined in the clutter, the Eameses weren't averse to it themselves, and ESU doubled as a display cabinet for decorative artefacts or as a bookcase-cum-room divider – another mid-century mini-trend.

In the 1950s, Jean Prouvé, Charlotte Perriand and Le Corbusier followed suit, designing cabinets along similar lines. Ponti also created a versatile sideboard crowned by a bookcase with open shelves.

Alternatively, household clutter could be neatly stashed away in that quintessentially mid-century piece, the beautifully crafted, sharply rectilinear sideboard (aka the credenza). This piece of furniture was phenomenally popular in Europe and Stateside, and was produced by G-Plan, Hans Wegner, Ilmari Tapiovaara and Florence Knoll, among many others.

LEFT **The crisply rectilinear sideboard, like this example by Robin Day, was many a mid-century homeowner's favourite storage unit.**

ABOVE **George Nelson's glass-topped sideboard from his 1950s Steel-frame furniture collection is as decorative as it is functional, thanks to the striking contrast between its enamelled metal frame and paler drawers.**

OPPOSITE **This mid-century desk incorporates plenty of storage yet avoids looking bulky thanks to its skeletal legs.**

George Nelson developed his 1940s Storagewall idea with his Comprehensive Storage System – or CSS – of 1959 for Herman Miller. This was versatile for being modular: standardized storage units and drawers could be swiftly slotted into its slim upright struts – and reconfigured. Style-conscious mid-century homeowners used storage units such as these as much for displaying decorative artefacts as for ordering their possessions.

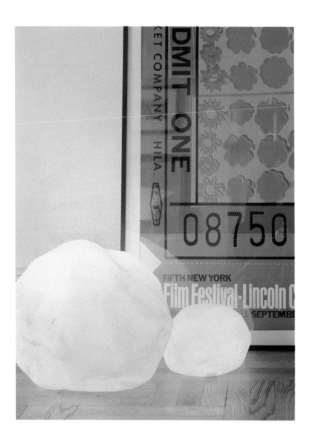

LIGHTING

 **OPPOSITE** Aside from designing furniture, architects John and Sylvia Reid created lighting for Rotaflex, including this 1950s floor lamp with a perforated metal shade, which casts an ambient light. Glare was anathema to mid-century lighting designers.

ABOVE Converted into floor lights, artist Piero Gilardi's rock-shaped Sedilsasso and Sassi seats of 1968 fuse mid-century ambient lighting with a Pop aesthetic.

ABOVE RIGHT Recalling Paco Rabanne's dresses, Verner Panton's glamorous 1960s Fun chandeliers conceal their light source behind clusters of shell discs.

RIGHT Achille and Pier Giacomo Castiglioni's asymmetric Snoopy light of 1967 boasts an eclectic mix of materials: marble, metal and glass.

Lighting was no less diverse than other areas of design, and greatly contributed to mid-century's overall eclecticism. If lighting was richly varied it was because it came in several mid-century styles, although it was predominantly organic-looking.

As well as favouring soft-contoured lighting, designers were determined to eliminate glare, believing this promoted a sense of wellbeing. Denmark's Poul Henningsen, who joined the country's

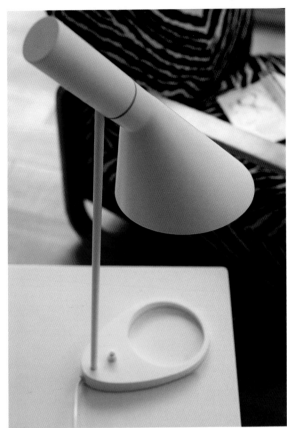

ABOVE LEFT A 1960s French floor lamp casts a warmly diffuse glow.

ABOVE RIGHT Arne Jacobsen's 1960 AJ table lamp was designed for his project the **SAS Royal Hotel in Copenhagen** and considered integral to its scheme. The hood-like shade's angle points directly downwards, avoiding glare.

LEFT A 1950s wall sconce by Serge Mouille illustrates the designer's witty use of black and white to connote light and shade.

OPPOSITE Inspired by a street lamp, Achille and Pier Giacomo Castiglioni's Arco floor light is just one example of the brothers' habit of taking inspiration from mass-produced objects when creating domestic designs.

leading lighting firm Louis Poulsen in 1925, had been researching this idea since the 1920s. His snowdrop-like PH5 lamp of 1958 – whose stacked shades diffused light – was an updated version of a lamp he originally designed in 1926. Like much mid-century design, the PH5 deployed modern materials – in this case sheet metal – to achieve its organic aesthetic.

In 1958, Henningsen dreamt up one of the most iconic – and baroque – lights of the 1950s: the Artichoke lamp incorporating cascading and overlapping copper 'leaves'

that generated a rich, tawny glow and obliterated any glare.

Glare was prevented by another key trend – simple, lantern-like shades that veiled their light source. In 1944, the Danish firm Le Klint began producing shades made of knife-pleated paper. In 1952, the Howard Miller Clock Company made George Nelson's Bubble lamps comprising a steel-wire cage spray-coated with transparent plastic. These had an organic, shape-shifting look: ranging from spheres to flying saucer shapes, they recalled the way soap bubbles morph into different forms when blown through a ring.

That same year, Isamu Noguchi created his ethereal Akari light, inspired by internally lit sculptures he had made in the 1930s and a period spent in Gifu in Japan, where he helped to revive its paper lantern industry as part of his contribution to rebuilding postwar-Japan's devastated economy.

OPPOSITE **Danish designer Nanna Ditzel's apartment in Copenhagen features one of Poul Henningsen's iconic pendant lights for Louis Poulsen. Determined from the 1920s onwards to devise soothing, glare-free lighting, Henningsen perfected his signature tiered shades in the '50s. These cleverly emit light horizontally, bathing surrounding walls in light.**

LEFT **A Henningsen table light similarly cuts out glare.**

ABOVE **Verner Panton's sleek 1971 Panthella lamp – whose shape recalls that of Eero Saarinen's Tulip furniture – was designed so that both its base and frosted acrylic shade reflect light evenly.**

LEFT AND OPPOSITE INSET **Noguchi's 1950s Akari lights are made of Shoji paper derived from mulberry tree bark, bamboo ribbing and a metal frame. 'Akari' in Japanese means illumination and physical lightness. 'The Akari's light is like the light of the sun filtered through Shoji paper,' noted Noguchi. 'The harshness of electricity is thus transformed through the magic of paper back to the light of our origin – the sun.'**

ABOVE LEFT **Poul Henningsen's majestic, multilayered Artichoke light of 1958.**

ABOVE RIGHT **Verner Panton's Moon light of 1960 comprises rings of plastic that hide the light bulb and serve as reflectors that cast a soft light.**

OPPOSITE **This George Nelson Bubble lamp stands on a metal tripod base but is also available as a pendant lamp.**

Fashioned from paper made from mulberry tree bark, his light married an ancient Japanese craft with Western modernism.

Italy, too, was a hotbed of lighting design. One of its most forward-thinking companies, Arteluce, was founded by aeronautical engineer and designer Gino Sarfatti, who was also inspired by modernist art: his 1953 2072 pendant light featuring disc-shaped shades in electric blue, yellow and red resembled a Calder mobile. Oluce, another visionary Italian firm, produced Joe Colombo's highly innovative 1962 space-age chic Acrilica lamp. This conducted light from a fluorescent element in its base and carried it up a C-shaped Perspex sheet that emitted an indirect glow.

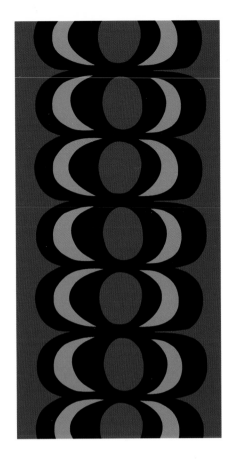

OPPOSITE A boldly abstract 1960s rug by Swiss company Teppichfabrik Melchnau. As the 1950s segued into the '60s, rug and textile design became much bolder.

RIGHT AND FAR RIGHT Few 1960s textile designs were as punchy as Marimekko's fabrics Kaivo on the left and the Warhol-esque Unikko, right, both created by designer Maija Isola in 1964. Inspired by American Expressionist painters like Frank Stella, Isola listened to music while designing, which she called 'dancing with the brush'. In the '60s, Marimekko designs were stocked by Habitat in London and Crate & Barrel in the US.

RUGS AND TEXTILES

Lucienne Day's Miró- and Klee-inspired linen fabric Calyx (see page 56) is both her best-known design and was one of the most internationally influential textiles of the 1950s. Manufactured by Heal's, it was exhibited at the Festival of Britain's Homes and Gardens Pavilion in a room designed by her husband Robin Day. In the same year, Calyx scooped a gold award at the Milan Triennale and, in 1952, the American Institute of Decorators' international design award, the first given to a British designer.

Its free-floating, semi-abstract pattern – suggestive of mushrooms and buttercups linked by nervy, spindly lines in lemon, vermilion, black and white against an olive ground – seemed to convey postwar Britain's tentative spirit of optimism. Yet its global success emboldened other textile designers to reference avant-garde art, and so helped democratize it.

British manufacturers Heal's, whose design department was led by the adventurous Tom Worthington, David Whitehead, Edinburgh Weavers and British Celanese – many of which commissioned artist-designed fabrics – were all initially at the vanguard of textile design. However, Britain was closely rivalled by Sweden, where Stig Lindberg had designed his boldly stylized Pottery fabric for department store Nordiska Kompaniet in 1947. Its vase motifs were autobiographical: they alluded to Lindberg's other role as a ceramicist, and highlighted the strong link in Sweden between textiles and ceramics that existed, too, in the UK.

Day also created patterns for Rosenthal ceramics and Terence Conran for David Whitehead and Midwinter.

In the 1950s, daring abstract textiles were designed by Paul McCobb for L Anton Maix in the US, Elsbeth Kupferoth for Pausa and Emtex in Germany and Gigi Tessari for JSA Busto Arsizio in Italy. Abstract fabrics were also popular as wall hangings, notably those by Verner Panton, also known for his bold, abstract-patterned rugs.

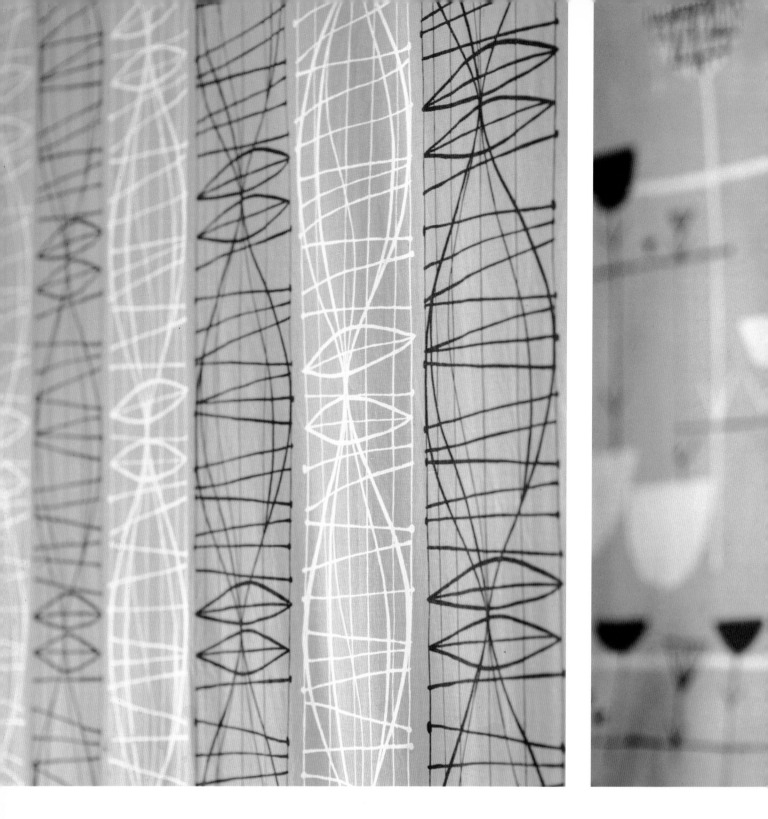

In the US, people who moved house frequently and left their fitted carpets behind bought into another mid-century micro-trend: the portable 'area rug', which was designed to define areas of activity within a room – a dining area, perhaps, or a TV corner. US-based designer Raymond Loewy catered to this with his geometric rugs for Edward Fields, which could cover most living-room floors.

ABOVE LEFT **A typically 1950s textile design whose print echoes the vogue then for spidery, linear imagery as well as modernist art, namely the sculptures of Naum Gabo, which incorporated stretched string, and the wiry sculptures of Lynn Chadwick, Eduardo Paolozzi and Reg Butler.**

ABOVE AND RIGHT **Marian Mahler emigrated to the UK in 1937, where she created her fabric Linear Flowers (above) in 1953 for David Whitehead, which also produced Maj Nilsson's fabric Haddon (right). Their spindly, naturalistic motifs were influenced by Lucienne Day's Calyx.**

OPPOSITE **Russel Wright's American Modern tableware ushered in a new curvilinear aesthetic in ceramics – a radical departure from Art Deco's jagged contours.**

RIGHT **Postwar West German ceramics, like these vases, made a major feature of glazes, just as studio potter Otto Natzler did in the US. German potters relished dripping, bubbling glazes in hues like sizzling orange and turquoise, and spawned a style called 'Fat Lava' wares. These were produced from the late 1950s to the '70s by such factories as Scheurich and Otto Keramik.**

BELOW **This vase is part of Italian company Bitossi's lustrous Rimini Blu collection, designed in the 1950s by its art director Aldo Londi.**

CERAMICS

Mid-century's roots lay not only in new developments in furniture but also in ceramics. Paralleling the trend for furniture of an organic bent championed by Alvar Aalto in Finland was a new taste for functional yet curvilinear ceramics trailblazed by Russel Wright and Eva Zeisel in the US.

Almost 10 years separated Wright's American Modern tableware of 1937 and Zeisel's similar, mass-produced Town and Country china of 1946 for US firm Red Wing Pottery, and Zeisel's was discernibly different. In place of Wright's murky, restricted palette and graceful teardrop shapes were her brighter, clashing hues, unstable-looking, floppier forms and also humour, in the form of anthropomorphic, almost cartoony salt and pepper shakers resembling a child nuzzling its mother.

Like many designers, Zeisel was inspired by contemporary art: Town and Country's biomorphic forms nodded to Arp and Moore; she herself noted that Salvador Dalí's images of melting watches helped shape the organic aesthetic of the 1940s. MoMA, too, egged on this swerve in taste, championing organic modernism and commissioning Zeisel's curvy, graceful Museum service of 1942.

A mix of mid-century and contemporary ceramics, including bowls on the far left by Gunnar Nylund, who was art director of Swedish firm Rörstrand, the main competitor to Gustavsberg, where Stig Lindberg had the same job in the 1950s. The shapes of Nylund's ceramics were ultra-organic and elemental.

INSET Ceramicist John Clappison's 1960 Home Decor vases for the UK's Hornsea Pottery, which were well known in the 1960s.

LEFT Hornsea Pottery's 1962 Summertime range came in typically 1950s jaunty white, black and yellow. Hornsea, which produced highly popular ceramics throughout the 1950s and '60s, was established by brothers Desmond and Colin Rawson. John Clappison was its chief designer from 1958.

BELOW Gunnar Nylund's trademark organic style is highlighted by these vases with slender, bird-like necks.

Yet organic ceramics were no ivory-tower phenomenon: American Modern sold over 80 million pieces from 1939 to 1959, thus propelling the style into the mainstream.

Mid-century ceramics also flourished in Britain, Italy, Germany, Finland, Sweden and Denmark, their hugely varied styles partly determined by the different infrastructures and traditions in place in each country. That said, handcrafted studio pottery – often intricately glazed or scored with *sgraffito* (decoration created by scratching an outer layer of slip to reveal a contrasting colour or tone underneath) – was popular and influential in all the aforementioned countries. Studio potters – such as US-based Gertrud and Otto Natzler, who admired the stonewares of Song Dynasty China, and the UK's Hans Coper, a fan of ancient Chinese bronzes – were often inspired by age-old cultures, producing work with a noticeably primitivist look.

Italy mainly specialized in small workshops and small-scale production and prized self-expression, often taken to madcap extremes. Picasso's Expressionist ceramics for Vallauris inspired the richly glazed, brazenly bizarre vases

of Guido Gambone and Marcello Fantoni. West Germany produced a sub-genre of ceramics called 'Fat Lava' wares – mottled, pitted pots dripping with igneous-looking glazes.

In Nordic countries, a limited number of manufacturers – Arabia and Iittala in Finland and Gustavsberg in Sweden, for example – favoured calmer, relatively minimalist ceramics, epitomized by Kaj Franck's 1948 clean-lined, practical, mix-and-match Kilta tableware for Arabia. In the UK, the most innovative ceramics were produced by Midwinter (see pages 20 and 62) and Poole Pottery (see page 36).

ABOVE LEFT AND RIGHT **When he was not experimenting with his pet motif – the leaf (see page 62) – Stig Lindberg sometimes created ceramics boasting zingy hues and graphic stripes, like this triple vase to the left and bowl, right, both for Gustavsberg.**

RIGHT **The idiosyncratic salt and pepper pots in Eva Zeisel's highly influential Town and Country tableware. These anthropomorphic pieces enact a kind of mother-and-child reunion, adding a dash of humour to her design.**

RIGHT Czechoslovakia's historic Bohemian glass industry was revived after the war by the new Communist government. Modernized factories exported new glass to bring in valuable foreign currency. Traditional styles were tossed aside by avant-garde glass artists like René Roubíček, who created this organic, gourd-shaped vase in 1964.

BELOW LEFT A 1959 stained-glass effect vase by Czech designer Vladimir Kopecky.

BELOW RIGHT Characteristically vibrant mid-century Italian vases.

OPPOSITE Decanters reminiscent of those by US company Blenko, renowned for its hand-blown glass in intensely jewel-bright shades.

OPPOSITE, INSET Graceful, candy-striped glassware by Venini, which commissioned cutting-edge designers from all over the world, including Tapio Wirkkala.

GLASS

Glass's malleability and potential to be juicily colourful greatly appealed to mid-century designers besotted with ultra-organic forms and a vibrant palette. Once again, Alvar Aalto – also a glass designer – set the pace with his free-form Aalto vase of 1936, co-designed with Aino Aalto and inspired by clothing worn by a Sami woman (an indigenous people of Arctic Scandinavia). A prototype was created by blowing glass into an irregularly contoured void between sticks impaled in the ground.

ABOVE **Designers in the 1950s and '60s drew attention to the affinity between glass and water with transparent or opaque pieces that came in myriad shades of blue, like a kingfisher's plumage. The 1960s Gulvase bottle by Holmegaard on the left and textured Banjo vase designed circa 1969 by Geoffrey Baxter for Whitefriars, right, are two examples.**

OPPOSITE, LEFT **Ingeborg Lundin's superbly simple Apple vase. Working for the Swedish company Orrefors from 1947, Lundin also designed engraved glass.**

The vase, whose form was reputedly influenced by the shapes of Finland's lakes, anticipated organic modernism's love of nature.

After the war, glass production thrived in Finland, Sweden, Denmark, Murano in Italy, Britain and Czechoslovakia; the latter only became internationally known when Czech glass was exhibited at the 1957 Milan Triennale. America's studio glass movement, meanwhile, was kick-started by Harvey Littleton in the late 1950s.

In Finland, the main glass companies were Iittala, Riihimaki and Nuutajärvi. Iittala's star designers were Tapio Wirkkala and Timo Sarpaneva. Wirkkala's fluidly organic Kantarelli vase (see page 13) and leaf-shaped bowls were a paean to nature. Sarpaneva also paid

RIGHT British glass designer Ronald Stennett-Willson created these vertebra-like Sheringham candleholders in 1967, the same year he opened his own factory in King's Lynn, Norfolk. He previously had a shop in London that sold contemporary Scandinavian and British glass and ceramics, and in 1958 penned the book 'The Beauty of Modern Glass'.

BOTTOM RIGHT A Holmegaard vase beside a plate by Lindberg for Gustavsberg.

homage to it literally – his Finlandia glassware was made using moulds of real bark (see page 21) – and in a more abstract fashion: he created his Orchid vase by injecting air pockets into solid crystal, and, by playing with chance, enhanced its organic look. In Sweden, at long-established factory Orrefors, designers Nils Landberg and Ingeborg Lundin represented nature in a highly abstract, pared-down, elegant way, he with graceful vases engraved with leaves, she with her proto-Pop Apple vase of 1957. Vicke Lindstrand, chief designer at high-profile Swedish glassworks Kosta, produced vases engraved with filigree-fine, linear images. And Per Lütken at Denmark's glass factory Holmegaard made gently asymmetric vases in limpid hues. Nordic glass hugely influenced the

whimsical work of British designers such as Geoffrey Baxter, who worked for leading manufacturer Whitefriars.

In stark contrast, Murano glass was kaleidoscopically colourful and anarchically patterned. It harnessed ancient decorative techniques, such as *murrine* (glass canes seen in cross-section), to create abstract, ultra-modern patterns. Murano company Venini had a cosmopolitan mindset, hiring foreign designers such as Wirkkala or creatives from other disciplines – like architect Tobia Scarpa and graphic designer Fulvio Bianconi – believing different perspectives stimulated fresh ideas.

Meanwhile, in Communist Czechoslovakia, where fine art was considered dangerously message-laden but glass apolitical, designers such as Jiří Harcuba and Pavel Hlava were free to create equally fantastical glassware.

METALWARE

ABOVE **This Campden tableware was co-designed in 1956 by British designers David Mellor and Robert Welch for stainless steel manufacturer Old Hall. Welch's studio was in Chipping Campden, Gloucestershire, hence its name. It won a Design Centre Award (given to designers in the UK) in 1958.**

OPPOSITE **Welch's starkly simple 1962 Alveston tea service for Old Hall, for whom he worked as a design consultant for 40 years. The range, which scooped a Design Council Award in 1965, included cutlery.**

utting-edge metalware took a two-pronged approach that chimed with mid-century's twin preoccupations: craft-orientated, organic-looking pieces on the one hand and avant-garde yet mass-produced, democratic designs on the other. Some silversmiths saw their craft as being on a par with fine art, and – in defiance of metal's unyielding, hard-edged qualities – created sculptural, organic, decorative pieces. Others simultaneously worked as industrial designers, since inexpensive steel and aluminium enabled them to make relatively affordable cutlery and tableware in a sleekly modern style.

Technological advances helped facilitate the latter: new aluminium and stainless steel alloys developed for industrial purposes during the war were available, by the 1950s, for use in the decorative arts.

And, with people increasingly hankering after labour-saving goods and informal lifestyles, these were coveted for being practical: unlike silver, they didn't tarnish.

The most innovative metalware producers were Britain, Denmark and France. London's Royal College of Art was a crucible of new ideas, and prominent metalworkers Gerald Benney, Robert Welch, David Mellor and Australian-born Stuart Devlin trained there before founding their own studios. The City of London's Worshipful Company of Goldsmiths also championed their designs.

TOP Mellor's 1958 Pride silver-plated tea set – he also designed an eponymous cutlery range – for Walker & Hall, which received a Design Council Award in 1959.

ABOVE From 1952, Danish designer Henning Koppel designed a series of covered dishes for serving fish or ragouts, like this Eel dish. Koppel, who trained as a sculptor, embarked on every new design in silver by making clay models.

RIGHT Koppel's sensual silver Pregnant Duck pitcher – its name spelt out its organic inspiration.

Welch and Mellor worked as both silversmiths and industrial designers. The former, whose aesthetic was influenced by modernist cutlery he had seen in Sweden, swung between producing elaborate pieces (like his Jackson Pollock-inspired candelabrum – see page 35) and more accessible cutlery for UK stainless-steel manufacturer Old Hall, including his minimalist 1962 design Alveston.

Welch and Mellor collaborated on the similarly pared-down tableware range Campden of 1956, made by Old Hall and Sheffield-based Walker & Hall. Born in Sheffield, the UK's stainless steel centre, Mellor studied metalwork at Sheffield College of Art. As a student, he designed his first cutlery set – the silver-plated Pride. Thereafter, his ultra-modern cutlery was made of stainless steel, including the

ABOVE RIGHT An uncharacteristically understated coffee set designed in 1959 by Stuart Devlin. Although ultra pared down, it has organic overtones, its beak-like spouts recalling long-necked birds. The pots, which have nylon bases, are free of handles that would interrupt their clean lines. Like many innovative metalware designers, Devlin trained under Professor Robert Gooden at London's RCA. He also made stainless steel cutlery for Sheffield-based firm Viners.

RIGHT An almost shoe-like teapot created by Devlin in 1963.

appealingly low-maintenance Symbol of 1962. This broke the mould of the era's standard 11-place setting ranges – commonly bought as wedding presents at the time – by comprising only eight pieces. More groundbreaking still was his ultra-democratic Thrift of 1965, which, whittled down to five multifunctional implements, was designed for hospitals, canteens and prisons. Meanwhile, Mellor's 1973 Provençal cutlery range with rosewood handles exemplified the organic makeover many mid-century designers gave metalware.

LEFT Cutlery doesn't get much simpler than this matt stainless steel, five-piece set designed by Arne Jacobsen for his SAS Royal Hotel in Copenhagen and manufactured by Georg Jensen. His super-streamlined design was used by the crew in the movie '2001: A Space Odyssey'.

BELOW LEFT A goblet by Stuart Devlin which, like many of his unashamedly decorative pieces, combined glistening silver and textured gold.

BELOW RIGHT David Mellor's first cutlery range, Pride, was designed in 1953 while he was a student at the RCA; it is still in production.

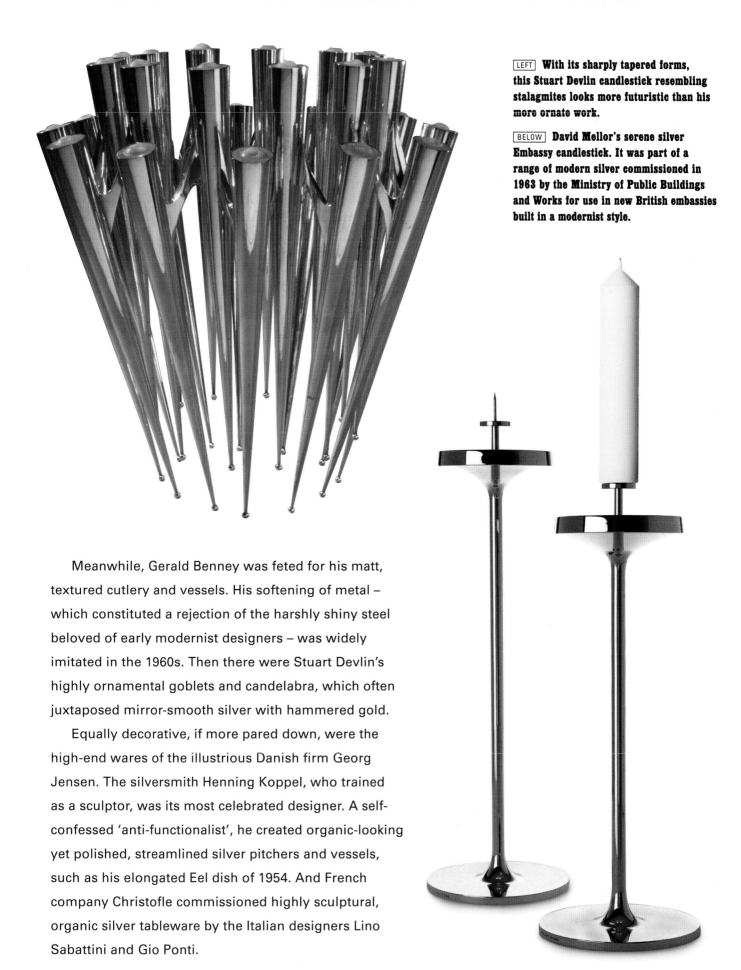

LEFT With its sharply tapered forms, this Stuart Devlin candlestick resembling stalagmites looks more futuristic than his more ornate work.

BELOW David Mellor's serene silver Embassy candlestick. It was part of a range of modern silver commissioned in 1963 by the Ministry of Public Buildings and Works for use in new British embassies built in a modernist style.

Meanwhile, Gerald Benney was feted for his matt, textured cutlery and vessels. His softening of metal – which constituted a rejection of the harshly shiny steel beloved of early modernist designers – was widely imitated in the 1960s. Then there were Stuart Devlin's highly ornamental goblets and candelabra, which often juxtaposed mirror-smooth silver with hammered gold.

Equally decorative, if more pared down, were the high-end wares of the illustrious Danish firm Georg Jensen. The silversmith Henning Koppel, who trained as a sculptor, was its most celebrated designer. A self-confessed 'anti-functionalist', he created organic-looking yet polished, streamlined silver pitchers and vessels, such as his elongated Eel dish of 1954. And French company Christofle commissioned highly sculptural, organic silver tableware by the Italian designers Lino Sabattini and Gio Ponti.

LIVING WITH MID-CENTURY COLLECTIBLES

The homes of mid-century architects and designers directly expressed their philosophy and taste. This chapter celebrates two stunningly stylish, highly original homes by titans of mid-century design Finn Juhl and Oscar Niemeyer. It also explores the homes of mid-century fans the world over, from a British beach house to modernist villas in Los Angeles and Sydney and a Palm Springs bungalow. Rather than shrines to mid-century, these homes are highly personal spaces that prove that the style is accessible and easy to live with.

HOLLYWOOD HILLS
HIDEAWAY

American architectural photographer Julius Shulman played a pivotal role in the Southern Californian mid-century movement. Via his books and exhibitions showcasing his super-glamorous images of the Case Study houses of Charles and Ray Eames, Pierre Koenig and Richard Neutra, he portrayed a thrustingly modern image of the mid-century style that's now internationally renowned.

He also snapped the Los Angeles houses of the less well-known yet prolific architect Carl Maston. These included the award-winning Maston – or Marmont – House, on Marmont Avenue in the Hollywood Hills, designed in 1947, and Hillside House on Sunset Strip. Incidentally, the latter's most recent owner restored it after chancing upon Shulman's photographs of it.

An economical palette
of materials creates a
cohesive look in the dining
room. The curves of its
custom-made dining table
by William Alexander and
Eames DCW chairs are
mirrored by the swirling
arabesques in the abstract
painting above them.
And a glass door opens
invitingly onto the
surrounding garden, which
boasts a swimming pool.

The Maston House is in the late American Craftsman style. Its sturdy, wood-framed exterior and strict adherence to natural materials, which give its interiors a satisfyingly unified look, epitomize this. An extension of Britain's Arts and Crafts Movement, the style took its name from the magazine *The Craftsman*, founded in 1901 by furniture maker and philosopher Gustav Stickley. Frank Lloyd Wright's Prairie School architectural style was an offshoot of this aesthetic, which reacted against ornate Victorian architecture and mass-produced housing, and championed robust structures, clean lines and locally handcrafted wood, glass and metalwork.

Born Carl Mastopietro in Illinois in 1915, Maston, who changed his name early in his career, studied music before settling on architecture at the University of Southern California. During World War II, he served as a Marine Corps transportation officer in Hawaii, but most of the fighting was over by the time he got there. Instead, he played tennis and daydreamed about building a house in LA – the future Maston House.

ABOVE AND RIGHT The restrained use of natural materials in one bedroom highlights the house's Craftsman style. It features a polished concrete floor that looks like stone and Wormley's chaise longue. Wormley's work was also shown at Chicago's Merchandise Mart between 1950 and 1955, alongside that of Harry Bertoia, George Nelson and the Eameses.

Returning to the city in 1946, Maston opened his first office in Beverly Hills and built the Pandora Apartments – one of his early experiments in garden apartment design (low-rise apartment blocks surrounded by landscaped grounds). He also designed university buildings and shopping centres. In 1960, he built the highly innovative Valley Ice Skating Center in Tarzana, California (demolished in the 1970s). Made of pre-cast concrete pieces that reinforced each other so that its wafer-thin, dramatically arching roof required no supporting columns, it was one of Maston's favourite projects. 'I couldn't go and watch it being torn down,' he said. 'It was like losing a baby.'

But Maston, who died in 1992, would surely be chuffed to hear that his eponymous house is alive and well. Architect Stephen Slan renovated it in the 1990s, even filling it with furniture in the mid-century style that Shulman's photographs famously immortalized.

In the living room are seminal, mid-century pieces, from a sideboard and table by Alvar Aalto – made by Finnish manufacturer Finnmar – to an Eames screen. The bas-relief wood sculpture is by artist Brian Willsher and the angular 'Constructivist' sculpture by the late artist Anthony Twentyman. The wall lamp behind is by Bestlite.

OPPOSITE The living room with a view of the hallway, with a 1940s chair by American architect Ralph Rapson and two clocks by George Nelson.

MID-CENTURY
MAGIC

The mid-century revival might be long established now, but it's largely thanks to London-based dealer and collector Andrew Weaving that it took off in the UK. When he started selling interwar furniture in Alfies Antique Market in London 20 years ago, most people regarded it as the design-world equivalent of a Martian – as in extremely odd. 'People just couldn't understand why I was selling it,' recalls Weaving, who is also co-author of *Modern Retro*, a seminal book on the subject. Today, his company Century sells mid-century design via www.centuryd.com.

In a guest bedroom are a totemic wood sculpture by Willsher, an Aalto chair and a stool inspired by the sculptures of Constantin Brancusi. On the shelves are ceramics by New Zealand-born Keith Murray, who designed for Wedgwood in the 1930s and '40s.

The long sofa in the living room was made in the 1920s for a house in the Bauhaus style in Stuttgart, Germany. Its owners moved to the UK in the 1930s, and brought it with them. Weaving bought it at auction house Phillips.

The living room is filled with daylight in the style of early modernist houses and furnished with armchairs designed for the same Stuttgart house as the sofa. There's also a languorous Marcel Breuer chaise longue and a re-edition of Egon Riis's 1930s Penguin Donkey bookshelf, both of which were designed for Isokon.

OPPOSITE, INSET This low-level table is by Aalto, the 1930s ceramics on it by French designer Jean Besnard. The white ceramics on the chest of drawers are by the mid-century-inspired, contemporary potter and designer Jonathan Adler, while the wooden screen is by the Eameses.

Some might have considered it perverse that Weaving persisted in stocking mid-century design at Alfies, but persist he did. 'Some collectors from Germany and Japan bought it, but it took ages to be taken seriously in the UK. At the time, anyone who was wealthy went for a more traditional style. In the late 1990s, I wrote and styled a story for *Elle Decoration* on modern furniture and from then on it started to be accepted.'

Aptly, this early adopter of mid-century especially likes the 1930s pieces of two early exponents of the style – Aalto and Breuer. Indeed, Weaving's weekend home on the Essex coast – a five-bed house designed by British modernist architect Oliver Hill and built in 1935 – is filled with Aalto's classic bent-ply pieces, from a sideboard to his better-known tables and stools. 'I like them because of their slightly crude quality, their simplicity,' explains Weaving, whose passion

for Aalto goes back a long, long way: he first became interested in him after seeing an exhibition on him at the Victoria and Albert Museum in London in 1987.

Weaving stumbled across his house while researching a book about mid-century. 'I looked at houses all round the country,' he says. 'This one, which *Country Life* magazine featured in a piece on modern country houses in 1935, is very near the sea. It had been empty for about 20 years, and I had to do a few internal redos but no major changes.' He's understating things, though: almost in violation of the modernists' love of daylight, the previous owner had bricked up doors leading to the garden and to several balconies. Obviously, Weaving immediately unblocked these. 'There was also a funny kitchen in the middle of the house and a small maid's room, but I knocked down their walls to open up the space,' he continues. 'And there was a very old-fashioned bathroom and separate lavatory that I converted into one room and modernized. The skirting/base boards

OPPOSITE Another view of the living room with an Aalto table and black-topped stools, Besnard ceramics, zebra-hide rug and, in the foreground, a Breuer chaise longue.

ABOVE A cluster of ceramics by Jonathan Adler adorn the top of an Aalto sideboard in the living room. The 1950s semi-abstract painting of a head behind them is by the British artist and writer John Banting.

RIGHT Weaving's arrangement of ceramics by Besnard seen in close-up. Their curvaceous forms perfectly complement Aalto's curvilinear furniture.

were all painted yellow and brown and there was lots of patterned wallpaper. I repainted the whole place white.'

Today, complementing Weaving's beloved Aalto furniture are other pieces in the same honey-toned mould – for example, chairs and serpentine screens by Charles and Ray Eames and a George Nelson chest of drawers and desk. The lighting, mainly Bestlite lamps, is starkly utilitarian. But despite this functionalist element, the emphasis here is on comfort – well, this is a weekend house, after all. And, of course, Aalto's bent-ply

LEFT The house's theme of honey-toned furniture is also in evidence in another bedroom, which is home to a George Nelson desk and an Eames chair. The lamp is by Isamu Noguchi.

BELOW In another bedroom, a wooden panel by Willsher sits on a shelf by Aalto. On an Aalto table is a Kaiser Idell lamp by Christian Dell, a designer at the Bauhaus.

OPPOSITE The bed, tray table and chest of drawers in the main bedroom are all by Nelson. The cushions are by Jonathan Adler, the tall, wooden sculpture by Twentyman.

furniture was supremely ergonomic. A sofa in the living room and a George Nelson bed in the main bedroom are strewn with plump cushions by designer Jonathan Adler, whose ceramics have channelled mid-century design since the 1990s; in fact, some adorn Weaving's Aalto sideboard. Two sunburst-shaped Nelson clocks strike a note of whimsy that makes the house feel more informal.

Not only was Weaving's early taste for mid-century vindicated long ago by the trend's popularity but it's now reached a mature, settled stage, he feels: 'A few years ago, people often bought it because it was fashionable, then moved on to the next big thing. But now people buy it because they genuinely like it and want to keep it. People remember their parents having it and that brings back good memories. Older stuff is usually made better, too. Buying it also fits in with our desire today to recycle things.'

ABOVE In the hallway are an Eames chair, a wood panel by Willsher, a planter by Californian company Architectural Pottery and a white abstract sculpture by Marinella Lawrence, a ceramic artist working today.

RIGHT Nesting tables by Breuer, designed for Isokon, and a Breuer chaise longue grace the living room. This 1920s music cabinet housed sheet music, and was made for the same German house that the armchairs in Weaving's living room were designed for. The TV is an original 1960s Sony set – the first-ever portable design.

OPPOSITE The furniture in the living room includes Isamu Noguchi's 1954 Cyclone table and a four-seater sofa, bought from Spence & Lyda and Orson & Blake respectively, two homeware shops in Sydney suburb Surry Hills. 'We wanted something comfortable for family life,' says Andrea about the sofa, while the large, elliptical Eames coffee table was chosen to complement the proportions of the 'oversized lounge'.

RIGHT On a terrace are two Butterfly chairs, a gift from a friend. The original design of 1935 is also known as the BKF chair after the initials of its designers Antonio Bonet, Juan Kurchan and Jorge Ferrari Hardoy. The coffee table is by Australian landscape architect and furniture designer William Dangar.

BELOW These armchairs were manufactured by Australian firm Danish Deluxe in the 1960s, and have been reupholstered in a dove grey fabric.

SEVENTIES STYLING

Andrea Millar and her husband Ben's passion for 1970s design, combined with their need for a larger home when their first son was born, led them to buy their beloved home, the ultra-modernist Turramurra House in Sydney's Upper North Shore area. 'A lack of space in our old Victorian terrace house meant a move was necessary,' recalls Andrea, an interiors journalist and stylist. 'I looked at three homes, but this one, which is 45 minutes' drive from the city, was the natural choice to me for modern living.'

This 1970s house, built on a huge slab of sandstone rock in bushland – uncultivated land covered with natural vegetation – reminded her of 'a building by iconic architect Frank Lloyd Wright, albeit a humbler version'.

RIGHT Another view of the living room, facing inwards. Swooping over the sofa is a flying saucer-shaped George Nelson lamp. On the floor is a geometric-patterned rug from Sydney store Koskela. The original Western red cedar wall that forms strong horizontal lines acts as a stylish backdrop to mid-century-esque Jonathan Adler ceramics and the Millars' collection of photos taken on trips to Uruguay (Andrea's country of birth), Cuba and Mexico. Art is used thoughout the house to inject pops of bright colour into the generally monochrome interiors. The abstract painting in joyous oranges and yellow is by Australian artist Stephen Ormandy and is from Sydney gallery Olsen Irwin.

Ben, an advertising director, and Andrea were also attracted to the house's open-plan layout, large living areas and floor-to-ceiling windows affording sweeping views of rugged countryside.

'I later realized the house was typical of an architecture movement kick-started in this area of Sydney in the 1950s, which was heavily influenced by Wright's principles of blending buildings with the landscape and of favouring natural materials. This would explain the use of earth-toned bricks inside the house and out, and the way Western red cedar clads many of the internal walls.'

Turramurra House, which had been rented for 30 long years before the Millars bought it, was in a sorry state and the couple renovated it extensively. 'Our vision was for an updated home that respected its period details, earthiness and simplicity,' recalls Andrea. 'But, where possible, we wanted to bring out the glamour and colour of the 1970s, with orange, pink and red highlights in the furnishings and art.'

The Millars first altered the kitchen's layout to allow it be easily seen from three surrounding areas: the dining room opposite, a TV room and a larger sitting room. In keeping with the house's original and restrained palette of natural materials,

the Millars added only four new finishes: Jura Grey limestone (a form of limestone adaptable to many uses) for floors and splashbacks, stainless steel for taps/faucets and appliances, easy-on-the-eye beige for the kitchen units and, finally, an element of graphic black in the form of a blackboard. The bathrooms were refurbished using similarly organic timber and stone.

While renovating the house, the Millars eagerly collected furniture that would help restore it to its former mid-century glory. 'We found our sofa, designed by Fred Lowen, and an Australian-made wood sideboard on eBay. Being children of the '70s, Ben and I bought them with nostalgia for our childhood and pride that we were recycling furniture.'

OPPOSITE In the dining area is a blackwood dining table with a linen table runner on it; both are from Sydney store Spence & Lyda. The ceramics are from Koskela, another Sydney store. The Eames chairs with 'Eiffel Tower' legs were bought from a second-hand furniture dealer, while the painting by David Band is from Sydney gallery Olsen Irwin.

ABOVE RIGHT In contrast to the house's busier mid-century style, the new, bespoke kitchen is contemporary and sleekly minimalist. The bold, horizontal lines of its Jura Grey limestone island echo those of the house's original cedar walls.

LEFT A neutral backdrop of cedar-lined walls in the TV room makes the juicy, watermelon pink upholstery of a sofa, designed by Fred Lowen for his company Fler (and bought on eBay), really sing. A fuchsia cowhide rug, from Australian company NSW Leather, adds another jolt of colour to the space.

OPPOSITE The floor lamp with a wooden base is from Sydney shop Orson & Blake, and while the original shade was also in brown, the Millars chose a white one to create a crisp contrast with the wooden wall behind it. The Kone chair by it was created in 1948 by Sydney-born designer Roger McLay. Made of a single sheet of bent plywood on steel-rod legs, it's a classic example of mid-century Australian design. The vintage sideboard was bought on eBay and the vases on it are by Australian brand Dinosaur Designs, one of whose creative directors is Stephen Ormandy, who painted the canvas in the Millars' living room. The sketch of a boy on the wall is by Cherry Hood and was bought from Sydney gallery Olsen Irwin.

The imminent birth of the Millars' second son galvanized them into carrying out some finishing touches. 'We plaster-boarded several brick walls in the bedrooms to provide visual relief from the grid-like pattern of exposed bricks,' says Andrea. 'And we landscaped some outdoor areas, taking care not to disturb the natural habitat of two Australian water dragon lizards that were almost pets to our older son.'

If one of the precepts of mid-century architecture is the blurring of indoors and out, Turramurra House is an authentic example of the style. By the sound of it, wherever the Millars are in their home, nature feels ever-present. 'We wake up every morning to the birdsong of the bush,' says Andrea. 'We know it's going to be a hot day when the kookaburras sing the loudest in the early hours.'

LEFT In the top-floor living room, original chest-high tongue-and-groove-covered walls in a rich linseed oil-like tone form a backdrop to a collection of vibrant ceramics and glass. The armchairs are by Robin Day, the daybed by Cappellini. The window leads onto a balcony.

ABOVE In the same room, Philippe Starck's Bubu stools stand by a traditional wood-burning stove by Danish company Rais.

ABOVE RIGHT A Rye Pottery blue and ochre jug with a typically attenuated mid-century silhouette sits on the bookcase.

BEACH-FRONT
BEAUTY

'About 20 years ago, friends of mine in Hastings told me that this house had come on the market,' remembers Philip Hooper, Design Director at prestigious London decorating firm Sibyl Colefax & John Fowler. 'They thought it needed someone to appreciate it and bring it back to life.' Easily persuaded, Hooper bought Beach House, as the house is called, soon after. 'It was designed in 1958 by architect Michael Patrick

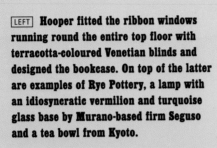

LEFT Hooper fitted the ribbon windows running round the entire top floor with terracotta-coloured Venetian blinds and designed the bookcase. On top of the latter are examples of Rye Pottery, a lamp with an idiosyncratic vermilion and turquoise glass base by Murano-based firm Seguso and a tea bowl from Kyoto.

RIGHT An arrangement of simple Poole Pottery vases with opaque turquoise and pale lime green glazes.

BELOW Decorative glassware, including a decanter striated with sulphur-yellow swirling stripes by Italian glassmaker Venini, adorns a corner of the living room.

for landowners who gravitated towards modern design. They still owned it when I bought it, and believed that Patrick hadn't built any other houses.'

Beach House is located just outside the English seaside town of Hastings in Sussex, and its boxy, flat-roofed, unornamented architecture is unusual for its surroundings. 'It's influenced by European modernism and Le Corbusier, although it has some English features,' says Hooper. 'It's partially clad in black weatherboarding that nods to the vernacular style of fishing huts on the Sussex and Kent coastline.'

In fact, Patrick's design makes maritime references aplenty. A jackknife-shaped staircase climbs its façade like stairs connecting a ship's decks. Indoors, an abundance of built-in furniture, mostly designed by a young Terence Conran, including crow's nest-like bunk

LEFT A glass, wood and brass 1950s desk by Silvio Berrone, made for the offices of Italian company Bialetti. The chair is by Italian designer Ico Parisi.

OPPOSITE Also in the living area are a sofa by David Hicks – interior designer to the international jet-set in the 1960s and '70s – a bookcase by Berrone, a '60s Italian lamp and a more recent painting by Gus Cummins. On the table, bought at a car-boot fair/fleamarket in Ohio, are chunky Ettore Sottsass ceramics.

beds and a typically mid-century ceiling-hung room-divider-cum-cabinet for storing glasses, evokes a ship's cabin.

Designed as a holiday home, the Beach House exudes a sense of fun, freedom and adventure. The living room – which boasts wraparound windows with zingy viridian frames – original dining area and kitchen occupy the top floor to make the most of the views, while the small bedrooms are situated on the first floor. Hooper rekindled the house's holiday spirit by converting a former carport on the ground floor into a new, alfresco dining area. This looks onto an outdoor space bristling with cacti, inspired by the Majorelle Garden in Marrakech, once owned by Yves Saint Laurent and his partner Pierre Bergé.

Discovering Beach House led Hooper to change his taste radically: previously he had a huge collection of Arts and Crafts design that was jettisoned in favour of mid-century classics. He conserved Beach House's original interiors, filling them with 1950s and '60s pieces – from Robin Day armchairs to painterly Poole Pottery ceramics and acid-bright Venetian glassware – as well as more recent furniture by Philippe Starck and Cappellini. Rather than recreate a mid-century aesthetic literally, Hooper's home shows that modern pieces can happily coexist with late 20th-century furnishings, creating a relaxed, comfortable air.

OPPOSITE **The living room with views
onto the swimming pool and garden.
The latter's greenery had been removed
in preparation for the house's demolition.
Present owners Michael and Gabrielle
Boyd replanted it with lush vegetation
in homage to the Brazilian landscape
architect Roberto Burle Marx, who
collaborated with Niemeyer. The glass-
fronted room reflects the desire among
many mid-century architects, such as John
Lautner, to fuse indoors and out and take
full advantage of panoramic views.**

ABOVE **Pieces here include George
Nelson's Marshmallow sofa – in an
unusual, all-white colourway – and
Frederick Kiesler's 1935 cast-aluminium
Two-Part nesting tables.**

ABOVE RIGHT **A typically mid-century
cabinet on a splayed-leg base.**

MODERNIST
MASTERWORK

The story of the Strick House in Santa Monica, California,
embodies the progressive, Left-leaning, mid-century mindset
to a T. The house was designed in 1964 for the Hollywood
film director Joseph Strick and his wife by the Brazilian
modernist Oscar Niemeyer, best known as the master architect of
Brasilia, which became Brazil's capital in 1960. Ironically, Niemeyer,
who died in 2012 aged 104, never saw the Strick house, and wouldn't
even accept a fee. A lifelong Communist, he was barred from entering
the United States several times, despite co-designing the United
Nations HQ in New York with Le Corbusier in the early 1950s. Strick
wrote to Niemeyer to say he was 'shocked and embarrassed' by this –
and commissioned him to design his home, the architect's one and
only residential project in the US.

Another view of the living room drives home its dramatic scale. The standout piece of furniture is a Mondrian-esque bookcase designed in 1952 by Charlotte Perriand, Jean Prouvé and Sonia Delaunay for the Maison du Mexique in Paris (part of the Cité Internationale Universitaire de Paris, which provides accommodation for students and academics). Otherwise the furniture is in sober neutrals. Vertical metal louvres fronting the windows provide shade from the bright Californian sunlight. One change the Boyds made was to replace linoleum floors in the living, dining and kitchen areas with palmwood, a nod to the buildings's Brazilian roots.

The dining area, which is part of the living room. The chairs are by Jean Prouvé, the ceiling light by Serge Mouille. Accents of colour in the mainly monochrome house are introduced by art, such as the abstract canvas by early 20th-century painter Burgoyne Diller, who was influenced by Piet Mondrian. The house was divided into a large living space and several, smaller bedrooms, as the Stricks had three children. This layout also suits the Boyds: 'Everyone has their private cocoon to retreat to, yet we can all come together in the centre, the main hub,' they say.

LEFT The house's media room, whose walls are appropriately decorated with vintage film, art and design posters. A lower ceiling, compared to that of the main living areas, inevitably creates a more intimate atmosphere suited to watching movies and TV, yet the mocha brown and white colour scheme found elsewhere continues here, too. A dramatically reclining LC4 chaise longue, designed in 1928 by Le Corbusier, Charlotte Perriand and Pierre Jeanneret, stands next to a window overlooking the garden, while Isamu Noguchi's 1944 coffee table occupies the centre of the room.

Communicating with his client by mail, Niemeyer designed the white brick and glass house by referring to aerial photographs, topographical plans, soil tests and input from Strick and his wife Anne, who requested a soaring ceiling in the communal spaces, a low one in the private areas and changes in level in the living area. Anne later said that their decision to commission Niemeyer was 'not only an aesthetic one but, in part, a way of thumbing our noses at the whole McCarthy era'.

After splitting with Joseph, Anne lived in the single-storey, flat-roofed, T-shaped house for 38 years. She eventually sold it to a developer who – oh the sacrilege! – planned to demolish it, although he discovered it was a landmark and so was unable to.

The house's current owners, mid-century enthusiasts Michael and Gabrielle Boyd, who have a consultancy for restoring and preserving modernist architecture and collecting modern art and design, bought the property in 2003 and spent the next two years restoring it. 'We were contacted about it back then, and at first we said: "There's no Niemeyer house in Santa Monica because, if there was, we'd have heard of it",' recalls Michael, who curated the design section of an exhibition called Birth of the Cool: California Art, Design and Culture at Midcentury that toured the US in 2007 and 2008.

The Strick House isn't typical of Niemeyer's aesthetic. One of Brazil's most prolific architects, he helped pioneer organic modernism: in 1954, he designed an outlandishly free-form, entirely curvilinear apartment block in Belo Horizonte in southeast Brazil. 'I'm not attracted to… straight lines,' he wrote in his memoirs. 'I'm attracted to

free-flowing, sensual curves. The curves I find in the mountains of my country, in the sinuousness of its rivers.' Yet the Strick House is rectilinear. Even so, its interior – encased by glass walls and comprising an open-plan living room combined with a dining room and kitchen, linked by a corridor to smaller bedrooms – is quintessentially mid-century.

For the Boyds, who have previously owned six modernist houses, including one in New York designed in 1975 by the Florida-based architect Paul Rudolph, the

ABOVE The base of the library – which contains a huge collection of books on 20th-century design – in the double-height living room; stairs lead up to a study. To create the lofty double-height space, the Boyds moved a garage out towards the street.

RIGHT The study is on a mezzanine level that provides access to books at a higher level. The Boyds' design-loving guests will happily spend all day there, studying its tomes. The seating is mainly by Jean Prouvé.

restoration of the Strick House proved to be a comparatively straightforward job. The main structural change they made was to remove a wall in what is now a double-height library (formerly divided into two bedrooms and a garage). The Stricks' décor had been flashy – imperial purple sofas and gold ceilings – and the Boyds stripped this away, but left some original features, such as a kitchen and pink marble bathtub, intact.

ABOVE AND LEFT A small study is home to a Jean Prouvé chair and Arne Jacobsen Swan armchair – just the tip of the iceberg in terms of the Boyds' vast mid-century furniture collection.

OPPOSITE, ABOVE AND BELOW A long corridor connects the spacious communal areas of the house with the smaller bedrooms, including the main bedroom, shown here. Above the bed hangs a painting by Japanese artist and writer Yayoi Kusama called 'Net Infinity', of 1959. A capacious George Nelson Coconut chair, which marries comfort with elegance, also graces the room, whose large sliding doors lead to the lushly planted garden.

They then filled the house with their swanky, extensive collection of furniture by Jean Prouvé, Gerrit Rietveld, Arne Jacobsen and Marcel Breuer, among others. This has been exhibited at the San Francisco Museum of Modern Art, yet the Boyds, who have two sons, don't treat their furniture like museum pieces but as an integral part of a busy family home. Sharing their parents' passion for mid-century, the sons own a white Verner Panton chair and an Eames desk chair.

Before he died, Oscar Niemeyer saw photos of the renovated house and emailed the Boyds to say he was thrilled.

FINN JUHL
Møbler og andre arbejder

KUNSTINDUSTRIMUSEET · BREDGADE 68 K
5. NOVEMBER - 5. DECEMBER 1982

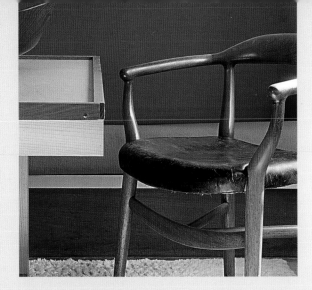

OPPOSITE The working area in the open-plan living room. Juhl – who studied architecture at the Royal Danish Academy of Fine Arts in Copenhagen, was apprenticed for 10 years to Danish architect Vilhelm Lauritzen, and opened his design studio in 1945 – also worked at his home. Most of the house's furniture was designed by him. Juhl's parents' home had been traditional, with leaded windows and repro furniture, and his spare aesthetic was in part a reaction against this.

ABOVE One of Juhl's chairs, which, with their gently sinuous contours, broke away from the rigidly geometric designs of his contemporary Kaare Klint.

RIGHT Avant-garde art was given equal prominence with design in Juhl's home.

SIMPLY
SCANDINAVIAN

Danish architect and designer Finn Juhl is perhaps less well known than his illustrious compatriots Arne Jacobsen and Verner Panton, yet he enjoys a cult following among mid-century buffs. Juhl's best-known design is the majestic teak and walnut Chieftain chair of 1949, which was exhibited at the annual Danish Cabinetmakers' Guild's exhibition that year. The story goes that King Frederick IX of Denmark tried it out, prompting a journalist to quip that it should be called 'The King's Chair' but, considering this too pretentious, Juhl dubbed it the Chieftain instead. The name reflected his passion for primitive sculptures, weapons and tools.

Juhl's pared-down furniture with its graceful curves and refined construction represented a radical break from Denmark's reigning fussy, classical style. He favoured cherry, maple, cedar, walnut and teak, and preferred wood to be rubbed lightly with oil rather than heavily varnished.

LEFT The working area in the living room. Cultured and widely travelled, Juhl installed a huge, built-in bookcase for his eclectic collection of books on a huge array of subjects from politics to art as well as fiction. Reading the spines of tomes in his home reveals names as wide-ranging as Simone de Beauvoir, Ibsen, Marc Chagall and Truman Capote. Juhl also favoured pale-coloured floors, such as in the living room, where the floor is made of unvarnished pine, and in the working area, which is covered with a cream rug.

ABOVE Juhl, who also created glassware, ceramics and even refrigerators (for US multinational General Electric), designed this cute, beautifully proportioned chest of drawers in a bedroom also used as an office by his wife Hanne. Manufactured by Baker Furniture, it's made of walnut and in two units pivoting on a vertical hinge so that they could be closed. The drawers, in graduated shades of blue and orange, yellow and red, are a perfect illustration of Juhl's predilection for flashes of colour. Colourful canvases like these are integral to the style of the house, and Juhl owned work by such avant-garde 20th-century artists as Asger Jorn (a founder member of the European art movement Cobra), Italian Futurist Gino Severini, Georges Braque and Pierre Soulages.

LEFT **The Chieftain chair in the light-filled living room.**

RIGHT **Also in the living room is Juhl's Poet sofa, designed in 1941 for his new home. The portrait – of Juhl's wife Hanne – demonstrates his love of accents of bright colour, as does the pink rug. Juhl liked designing low-level tables, like these ones, as he thought they looked more informal. The table light was designed by Lauritzen. The other painting is by Richard Mortensen. A plant-filled 'garden room' can be glimpsed at the far end. Indeed, Juhl, who liked transparency in interiors, designed his home so that each room flows into another. In the garden room, this is enhanced by a glass cabinet – a room divider that doesn't block out light.**

In his heyday – the 1950s and '60s – Juhl was internationally feted: he scooped five gold medals at the Milan Triennials. In 1950, he designed the interior of the Trusteeship Council Chamber at the United Nations headquarters in New York, while in 1960 his work was showcased in an exhibition at the city's Metropolitan Museum of Art entitled The Arts of Denmark.

His furniture was often originally designed for his home and the Chieftain and other Juhl pieces can be seen at the house he built in 1942 in Ordrup, a suburb of Copenhagen, which, kept intact since he died in 1989, has been a museum since 2008. This house, where he lived with his second wife Hanne Wilhelm Hansen, a music publisher, is an early example of an open-plan interior. Juhl designed the building from the inside out, its internal layout determining the house's exterior form.

Juhl wanted his home to have a feeling of transparency, of the indoors blending with the outdoors. He had some ground excavated on the site to form a shallow bowl that the house stands in, so that the sloping garden around it can be seen and appreciated at close range. He also designed a large glass window that spans most of the huge living room, which also incorporates a work area and library. The house comprises two parallel blocks. One holds a large living room and a small study, in the other are the kitchen, dining room, bedrooms and bathroom. These two blocks are joined by an entrance hall that opens onto the garden.

Juhl's approach to interior design was rational – his almost spartan kitchen was designed to be ultra-practical and labour-saving – yet playful. He liked to offset his use of natural materials with pops of brighter colour, painting the ceiling of each room in his house a different hue to create subtly contrasting moods. In the living room, a warm parchment shade on a sloping ceiling simulates the effect of being under a tent with the sun shining through.

He also saw the house as a *Gesamtkunstwerk* – the German term for a complete artwork – and designed everything in it, right down to the trays and crockery. Juhl was hugely inspired by modernist art, and believed there was a natural crossover between avant-garde art and design. His home was filled with sculptures and paintings.

Juhl may not be a titan of 20th-century Danish design but – well travelled and well connected – he was highly instrumental in putting it firmly on the map.

OPPOSITE Another Juhl chair, of 1953, manufactured by Danish firm Bovirke. A shelf atop the backrest is designed to be used as an armrest if you're sitting at a certain angle. Juhl's pieces were meticulously crafted by cabinetmaker Niels Vodder; they collaborated for many years. His furniture was also popular in the US, where it was made by American manufacturer Baker Furniture.

Juhl's FJ48 settee and armchairs with teak frames and caramel-coloured leather upholstery, designed in 1948. Juhl often created his settee designs – like this one – by duplicating a chair. In 1949, following this principle, he also created his Double Chieftain sofa. A hallmark of Juhl's furniture is that the seat and backrest are separated slightly from the frame.

ABOVE In the living area are a 1960s sofa and chairs by Florence Knoll bought from a shop specializing in mid-century in Michigan years before the house was built. Grasscloth wallpaper provides texture, while custom-built cabinetry echoes similar mid-century designs.

OPPOSITE In front of a wall hung with family photos in the office are a vintage Eames rocker with an apple-green seat, Eames LCM chair, Eero Saarinen table and lamp with fibreglass shades.

RIGHT In a sitting area are a lipstick-red Eames DCW chair with a rare aniline-dye finish and a wall-hung moulded plywood splint originally designed by the Eameses for the US Navy in the 1940s.

MID-CENTURY
REVISITED

Few people can have been as precocious as American-born Sean Brunson was when he began buying mid-century pieces. 'I started collecting them in my teens,' remembers Brunson, an associate creative director at an advertising agency in Orlando, Florida. 'Back then, in the late 1980s/early 1990s, they were far cheaper – you could buy an Eames chair for $20 at a thrift store.' Before this, family connections had instilled in Brunson a love of mid-century design, a lifelong passion that even saw him commission his home – a new-build house in Orlando – in this style.

In the dining area are vintage Eames, walnut dining chairs,
a table Brunson made by combining second-hand table legs
with a new plank of wood for the top and a George Nelson
lamp from Modernica, a shop in Los Angeles.

OPPOSITE Another view of the dining area, where a wall running through the house to the garden bridges indoors and out. The wall-hung cabinet was custom-built. In the courtyard, used for alfresco meals, are a vintage table by Richard Schultz and chairs by Harry Bertoia.

RIGHT In the sitting area are an Eames Lounge Chair and Ottoman and a coffee table. The fireplace was raised off the ground so that it appears to float.

When he was a child, family friends owned a house designed by Paul Rudolph, the best-known figure of the Sarasota School of Architecture, a Florida-based offshoot of the mid-century architecture movement. 'I had the privilege of holidaying there and, although I didn't realize it then, this had a major influence on my life,' Brunson recalls. 'Sarasota Modern, as it's also known, is often compared with California's Case Study houses.' The first of these branches of mid-century architecture was active from 1941 to 1966, the second from 1945 to 1966. The Sarasota style of architecture responded to climatic conditions, with buildings incorporating broad overhangs to shield them from strong sunlight and jalousie windows (with louvred glass slats that open). They also often featured floating staircases with cantilevered stair treads.

Another leading name from the Sarasota School was Gene Leedy. Such was Brunson's passion for its aesthetic that he hired Leedy to design the concept for his four-bed, single-storey house, later completed by local architect Alex Stone. 'I wanted it to be true to the modern spirit with the biggest space being the

living room – incorporating a kitchen and dining room – and smaller bedrooms,' says Brunson. 'I wanted that feeling of inside/outside living, too, created by long glass walls.' The resulting design indeed boasts a spacious living area. Light permeates the house through a glass wall running along the back of the house and glass doors leading to all the bedrooms, which also have access to the garden.

Another hallmark of the Sarasota style – found, too, in Brunson's house – are external walls made of concrete blocks that invade the house's interior, helping to bridge indoors and out. 'These make a feature of the joints, and the mortar between them has to be inserted at a consistent depth – a technique called "raking",' says Brunson. 'It was a challenge finding a company that could do this. In a pared-down design, great care has to be paid to details. Any imperfections show up easily.'

Appropriately, Brunson filled its authentically American mid-century interior with mainly US pieces. 'The work of Florence Knoll, George Nelson and Paul McCobb in particular really touches my heart. The Eameses, too, were an amazing team. Their talents blow me away.'

Sunshine yellow accents – in the form of two 50s Eames armchairs and a vibrant abstract painting – enliven one of the guest bedrooms. Florence Knoll's Credenza cabinet stands in the foreground. The room also cleverly plays with scale: forming a graceful arc, a vintage lamp towers above a dinky Eames LTR table and an oh-so-1950s Swiss cheese plant.

Buyers should not be put off by worn-looking pieces such as this Eames Lounge chair with its lived-in, conker-brown, leather upholstery. Indeed, many dealers believe that age and character are highly desirable.

Bertoia's Diamond chair for Knoll (above left) and Nelson's Coconut chair for Herman Miller (right) represent sound investments since these manufacturers, along with Carl Hansen & Son, PP Møbler and Fritz Hansen, produced supremely iconic designs. The same can be said for Eames, Wegner and Race pieces, which are as popular today as they were 60 years ago.

HOW AND WHAT TO BUY

One reason why mid-century appeals to so many is its sheer variety. Yet this can also make buying and collecting it seem daunting. How can a collector get started? Pieces by lesser-known names can be just as desirable as those by stellar designers, but what should collectors look out for? How can buyers sift the good from the bad, originals from fakes?

Yet it needn't be scary, since one widely respected good rule of thumb is to follow your own personal taste: 'Buy what you like,' urges Andrew Weaving, the high-profile yet laid-back mid-century dealer whose own house is featured on pages 152–163, and who picks up pieces for a song in thrift shops and garage sales in the US. 'On American mid-century blogs, people enthuse about colours, shapes, a look or style rather than names. There's no snobbery attached to it.'

If you're buying for yourself, a piece's authenticity – and condition – aren't crucial, he believes: 'I have a lot of Keith Murray Wedgwood china with chips in it. One without a chip can cost £1,000, one with £100. So much mid-century is reproduced now that the line between fakes and originals is becoming increasingly blurred. And some companies such as the Murano firm Seguso didn't sign their pieces.'

Meanwhile, Lucy Ryder Richardson, the co-founder with Petra Curtis of the popular Midcentury Modern selling exhibitions and The Midcentury Modern Marketplace, a stockists' directory, offers some useful tips. 'If you're buying something expensive, stick with reputable dealers. It helps to research the dates and producers of pieces you like – unless you love them no matter what – so that you can see if these correspond with the details on a dealer's label. When buying a piece from a shop or fair, ask the dealer to write as much information as possible about it on the receipt – its age, designer, date. The receipt adds great value to it. And ask the dealers if a piece is original. You can sometimes tell if pieces are original by inspecting them: most Eames rockers have new bases.' One indication of authenticity is 'signs of wear', she adds. 'Avoid over-restored pieces.'

'If you're buying reproductions,' Ryder Richardson continues, 'the nearer the date of the item's production to that of the original the better. Avoid pieces that have recently gone into production again. The minute I saw that my quite rare bar stools by Danish designer Erik Buck – like those in Don Draper's apartment in [the TV series] *Mad Men* – were going into production again, I was gutted because reproductions can devalue originals.'

For those people who are able to afford high-end, iconic mid-century pieces – whether new or old – establishing authenticity is very important, says Tony Ash, the MD in the UK of Vitra. 'What people should look for in design classics still in production is authenticity. Buy authorized pieces from licensed manufacturers

TOP George Nelson's Bubble light is still in production today. When buying reproductions, the best approach is to look out for examples that were made as near as possible to the date of the original piece.

ABOVE Lesser-known names, such as Denmark's Jens Quistgaard, are also worth collecting. Quistgaard created this teak ice bucket, inspired by a Viking ship's hull, in the 1960s for the US firm Dansk Designs.

OPPOSITE Arne Jacobsen's 4130 chair of 1957 is highly sought-after, as it has never been reissued.

such as Vitra, Knoll and Cassina, as these will always have value. Cheap copies from China are worthless.'

Websites such as eBay, fairs and car-boot or yard sales can also be good sources of mid-century, but they do have their pros and cons. 'The joy of buying online is the speed with which you can source things and the chance you have to research them before you commit to buying them,' says Petra Curtis. 'The downside is the risk of buying a fake, although if you buy one using Paypal you can get your money back. With fairs and car-boot sales, there's the thrill of discovering a piece. And you can talk to the seller and handle and check pieces.'

Andrew Weaving – a huge fan of America's Goodwill thrift stores and its auction website shopgoodwill.com – agrees that it's best to see and handle pieces. 'Fake Eames chairs, for example, are feather-light.'

Fashions in mid-century change – and what's sought-after is subjective – but some constants apply when collecting it. Curtis puts her money on 'manufacturers Herman Miller, Carl Hansen, PP Møbler and Knoll, which produced some of the most iconic designs, and designers Børge Mogensen, Hans Wegner, the Eameses, George Nelson and Ernest Race, whose pieces are timeless'. And lesser-known names? Ryder Richardson suggests Tapio Wirkkala, Danish designer Jens Quistgaard, German designer Dieter Rams's products for Braun, 'which inspired Apple's designer Jonathan Ive', and the work of women designers, such as Denmark's Grete Jalk, which is still 'massively underrated'.

Weaving recommends the mass-produced furniture of US firms Drexel and Broyhill – 'in plentiful supply, as every department store in America stocked it' – aluminium wares by the firm Kensington and US-based designer Georges Briard's Fornasetti-esque glassware. 'In the UK, most of John and Sylvia Reid's designs for Stag Furniture are reasonably affordable,' he adds.

True, collecting from scratch involves a bit of a learning curve, but mid-century needn't be a minefield.

OPPOSITE A stellar line-up of must-have pieces by heavyweight mid-century designers – Norman Cherner's Cherner chairs, a Saarinen table, Isamu Noguchi coffee table, and Eames chair and table in the foreground.

ABOVE AND TOP Tapio Wirkkala, who created this vase and geometric 1970s Polygon tea service for Rosenthal, is a lesser-known designer whose work is highly regarded by collectors, according to Lucy Ryder Richardson, co-founder of the UK's Midcentury Modern selling exhibitions.

SOURCES

UK

ALFIE'S ANTIQUES MARKET

13–25 Church Street
London NW8 8DT
020 7723 6066

www.alfiesantiques.com

London's largest indoor market
for antiques, collectibles and
20th-century design treasures.

ARAM

110 Drury Lane
London WC2B 5SG
020 7557 7557

www.aram.co.uk

Founded 50 years ago by Zeev
Aram, the Aram store still stocks
modern classics by a huge range
of designers, from Alvar Aalto to
Hans Wegner.

ARTEMIDE

106 Great Russell Street
London WC1B 3NB
020 7291 3853

www.artemide.com

Modern Italian lighting.
Artemide's earliest design,
Alfa (1959) by Sergio Mazza,
is still available, along with
other modern pieces such
as Eclisse (1967) by Vico
Magistretti, and Pipe (2004)
by Herzog & de Meuron.

CENTURY

www.centuryd.com

Dealer and collector Andrew
Weaving owns this gallery
specializing in British and
American mid-century classics
by Robin Day, Lucian Ercolani,
Charles Eames, George Nelson,
John and Silvia Reid, and others.
Also new production of Eames
fibreglass chairs, Nelson bubble
lamps, and Noguchi dining and
side tables.

CHAPLINS

477–507 Uxbridge Road
Hatch End, Pinner
Middlesex HA5 4JS
020 8421 1779

www.chaplins.co.uk

A wide range of original items
and new furniture inspired by
mid-century designs.

COTSWOLD VINTAGE & RETRO

07525 050977
07872 532145

www.cotswoldvintageandretro.com

Restored mid-century originals
at competitive prices.

DECOTRADE

66 Roseville Road
Leeds LS8 5DR
0113 414 8307

www.decotrade.co.uk

A selection of 20th-century design
originals.

DESIGNS OF MODERNITY

Crystal Palace Antiques & Modern
Jasper Road
London SE19 1SG
07966 285694

designsofmodernity.com

Mid-century furniture, lighting
and metalware.

ERCOL

01844 271800

www.ercol.com

Manufacturer of timeless wooden
furniture for almost a century,
including the famous Loveseat
(1956) and Butterfly chair. Visit
the website for details of a
stockist near you.

FANDANGO INTERIORS

2 Cross Street
London N1 2BL
07979 650805

www.fandangointeriors.co.uk

Mid-century modern furniture,
lighting and accessories.

ESTHER FITZGERALD RARE TEXTILES

28 Church Row
London NW3 6UP
020 7431 3076

www.estherfitzgerald.com

Vintage 20th-century textiles.

ETSY

www.etsy.com

Online marketplace for handmade
goods and vintage items.

1STDIBS

www.1stdibs.com

International online marketplace
inspired by the Marché aux Puces
in Paris, bringing together more
than 1,500 dealers in antiques,
vintage furniture and design.

FASHION FOR HOME

www.fashionforhome.co.uk

Online store selling modern
Scandinavian furniture based on
classic designs.

FEARS AND KAHN

Unit 4, Criftin Enterprise Centre
Oxton Road, Epperstone
Nottinghamshire NG14 6AT
01949 851 736

www.fearsandkahn.com

Vintage furniture, lighting and
decorative objects. Viewings by
appointment only.

FUNKY JUNKY

4a The Maltings
Railway Place
Hertford SG13 7JT
07970 265822

funky-junky.co.uk

Utility furniture from the 1950s to
the 1970s, and classic pieces from
designers such as Arne Jacobsen,
Robin Day and Vernon Panton.

GALLERY 25

26 Pimlico Road
London SW1W 8JL
020 7730 7516

www.gallery25.co.uk

Original 20th-century decorative
designs including tables, chairs,
mirrors, chandeliers and wall
lighting.

INTERIOR ADDICT

50–52 Commercial Street
London E1 6LT
020 7377 1855

www.interioraddict.com

Reproductions of design classics
at good prices.

LOVELY & CO.

Unit 5, Davigdor Mews
Hove
East Sussex BN3 1RF
07976 931671

www.lovelyandcompany.co.uk

Online vintage furniture store.
Workshops and showroom near
Brighton can be visited by
appointment.

MAC & MAC INTERIORS

35–42 East Street
Farnham
Surrey GU9 7SW
01252 717771

www.macandmacinteriors.co.uk

Huge range of contemporary
European designer furniture,
lighting and accessories.

MARIMEKKO

16–17 St Christopher's Place
London W1U 1NZ
020 7486 6454

www.marimekko.com

Tableware and household textiles
in bold Scandinavian designs.
Outlets throughout the UK.

MID-CENTURY ONLINE

www.mid-centuryonline.com

Online shop selling mid-century
furniture, especially chairs, tables,
desks, sofas and lamps.

THE MODERN HOME

777 Warwick Road
Birmingham B11 2HA
0845 475 5049
0121 707 0124

www.themodernhome.co.uk

Specialists in good-value modern
furniture based on classic mid-
century designs.

THE MODERN WAREHOUSE

3 Trafalgar Mews
London E9 5JG
020 8986 0740

www.themodernwarehouse.com

Original vintage pieces; viewing
by appointment.

PLANET BAZAAR

Arch 68, The Stables Market
Chalk Farm Road
London NW1 8AH
020 7485 6000

www.planetbazaar.co.uk

Vintage and collectible furniture,
lighting, art and accessories.

SCP

135 Curtain Road
London EC2A 3BX
020 7739 1869
and at
87 Westbourne Grove
London W2 4UL
020 7229 3612

www.scp.co.uk

Manufacturer and retailer
of a wide range of modern
furniture, lighting and
accessories, both vintage
and new designs.

SKANDIUM

245–49 Brompton Road
London SW3 2EP
020 7584 2066
and 86 Marylebone High Street
London W1U 4QS
020 7935 2077

www.skandium.com

Scandinavian furniture, lighting,
ceramics, glass, textiles and rugs.

SKINFLINT DESIGN

01326 565227

www.skinflintdesign.co.uk

Online store selling reclaimed
retro lighting and salvaged lights
from the 20th century.

THEMES AND VARIATIONS

231 Westbourne Grove
London W11 2SE
020 7727 5531

www.themesandvariations.com

Mid-century modern and
contemporary design with
a focus on Scandinavian
and Italian furniture and
decorative arts.

TOJO DESIGN

The Lighthouse
11 Mitchell Lane
Glasgow G1 3NU
0141 248 2824

www.tojodesign.com

Mid-century furniture and lighting
originals.

TWO COLUMBIA RD

2 Columbia Road
London E2 7NN
020 7729 9933

www.twocolumbiaroad.co.uk

Collectible furniture by designers
such as Hans Wegner, Finn Juhl,
Arne Vodder, Joe Colombo,
Ettore Sottsass, Charles Eames
and Poul Kjaerholm.

VESSEL

114 Kensington Park Road
London W11 2PW
020 7727 8001

www.vesselgallery.com

Ceramics and glass, both vintage
and new.

VINTAGE RETRO

07711 408960
07715 054919

www.vintageretro.co.uk

Online store specializing in
vintage retro furniture and
household accessories, with a
warehouse in Jarrow, Tyne &
Wear, that can be visited
by appointment.

US and CANADA

B&B ITALIA USA

150 East 58th Street
New York, NY 10155
800-872-1697

www.bebitalia.it

Top-quality Italian furniture from a company at the forefront of innovative technologies for 50 years. More than 800 sales outlets worldwide.

BOOMERANG FOR MODERN

2475 Kettner Boulevard
San Diego, CA 92101
619-239-2040

www.boomerangformodern.com

Classic mid-century modern furnishings, lighting and accessories. Most are vintage; some are new from the original manufacturers and craftspeople.

CASSINA USA

155 East 56th Street
New York, NY 10022
212-245-2121
and 151 Wooster Street
New York, NY 10012
212-228-8186

www.cassinausa.com

Reissues of many iconic pieces of modern design.

CHARTREUSE MODERN

2609 First Avenue
Seattle, WA 98121
206-328-4844

www.chartreusemodern.com

Selection of original 20th-century classics plus modern reissues.

CHRISTOPHER FARR USA INC.

748 N. La Cienega Boulevard
Los Angeles, CA 90069
310-967-0064

www.christopherfarr.com

Contemporary rugs and textiles using the best available yarns, dyes and weavers.

CIRCA 50

www.circa50.com

Online store offering reissues by modern designers as well as vintage tableware, lighting and storage.

DESIGN WITHIN REACH

www.dwr.com

Examples of iconic works in production since the mid-20th century as well as innovative new items. Buy online or visit one of the 30-plus studios nationwide.

DONZELLA 20TH CENTURY GALLERY

17 White Street
New York, NY 10013
212-965-8919

www.donzella.com

Modern 20th-century pieces, with an emphasis on American and lesser-known Italian designers.

ETSY

www.etsy.com

Online marketplace for handmade goods and vintage items that aims to encourage small-scale craft entrepreneurship.

1STDIBS

www.1stdibs.com

International online marketplace inspired by the Marché aux Puces in Paris, bringing together more than 1,500 dealers in antiques, vintage furniture and design.

FULL HOUSE

428 Northampton Street
Easton, PA 18042
610-258-9330

www.fullhouse20.com

Original 20th-century furniture.

GOMOD

www.gomod.com

Online marketplace for buyers and sellers of mid-century modern design.

HIVE

www.hivemodern.com

Internet superstore of 20th-century design, offering both new and vintage pieces.

I LIKE MIKE'S

161 Decature Street
Brooklyn, NY 11233
917-562-0292

www.mikesmcm.com

Restored vintage and mid-century modern furnishings and lighting.

INFORM INTERIORS

50 Water Street
Vancouver, British Columbia
Canada V6B 1A1
604-682-3868

www.informinteriors.com

Reissues of modern classics, as well as many contemporary pieces.

JONATHAN ADLER

www.jonathanadler.com

Potter and designer Jonathan Adler creates contemporary ceramics with a retro sensibility. His work is now available at 26 stores nationwide.

LOST CITY ARTS

18 Cooper Square
New York, NY 10018
212-375-0500

www.lostcityarts.com

Original and reissued design classics.

MACHINE AGE

645 Summer Street,
Boston, MA 02210
617-464-0099

www.machine-age.com

New England's largest selection of mid-20th-century furniture.

MARIMEKKO

200 Fifth Avenue
New York, NY 10011
212-843-9121

www.marimekko.com

Tableware and household textiles in bold Scandinavian designs. Outlets nationwide.

MIDCENTURY MODERN FINDS

415-606-6508

www.midcenturymodernfinds.com

Online dealer in vintage furniture and accessories, based in San Francisco, CA.

MODE MODERNE

159 North 3rd Street
Philadelphia, PA 19106
215-627-0299

www.modemoderne.com

Selected pieces by Arne Jacobsen, Florence Knoll and others.

MODERN CLASSICS FURNITURE

PO Box 31397
Bellingham, WA 98228
360-733-6400

www.modernclassics.com

Reproductions of Scandinavian and mid-century modern furniture, all made by hand from high-quality, eco-friendly materials.

MODERNICA

57 Greene Street
New York, NY 10012
212-219-1303
and at 7366 Beverly Blvd
Los Angeles, CA 90036
323-933-0383

www.modernica.net

Modern classics as well as Modernica's own range of contemporary pieces. Showroom in Los Angeles.

MODERN TIMES

2100 West Grand Avenue
Chicago, IL 60612
312-243-5706

www.moderntimeschicago.com

Mid-20th-century furnishings, lighting and decorative objects.

MODERN WAY

745 North Palm Canyon Drive
Palm Springs, CA 92262
760-320-5455

www.psmodernway.com

Carefully chosen pieces from the 1940s to the 1970s.

NJ MODERN

200 South Newman Street
Hackensack, NJ 07601
201-342-3245

www.njmodern.com

Made-to-order reproductions of mid-century modern furniture.

QUASI MODO

789 Queen Street
West Toronto
Ontario M6J IGI
416-703-8300

www.quasimodomodern.com

Modern furniture by a wide range of renowned designers.

REGENERATION

38 Renwick Street
New York, NY 10013
212-741-2102
and at
ABC Carpet & Home
888 Broadway
New York, NY 10003
212-473-3000

www.regenerationfurniture.com

Features some of the best early examples of Florence Knoll, Jens Risom, Paul McCobb, Edward Wormley, George Nelson, Harvey Probber and Milo Baughman.

REVOLVE MODERN

163 Howell Street
Dallas, TX 75207
469-867-8360

www.revolvemodern.com

Mid-century modern chairs, tables and storage.

ROOM & BOARD

800-301-9720

www.roomandboard.com

Retro-inspired contemporary furniture. Buy online or from one of 14 retail outlets nationwide.

SENZATEMPO

1655 Meridian Avenue
Miami Beach
FL 33139
305-534-5588

www.senzatempo.com

Designer furniture dating from 1930 to 1960, located in the art deco district of Miami Beach.

THRIVE HOME FURNISHINGS

8110 Beverly Boulevard
Los Angeles, CA 90048
323-944-0669

www.thrivefurniture.com

Online store selling reproduction sofas and seating. Showroom in Los Angeles.

VANGUARD FURNITURE

109 Simpson Street
Conover, NC 28613
828-328-5601

www.vanguardfurniture.com

Vanguard's Michael Weiss collection is based on mid-century originals.

WEST ELM

888-922-4119

www.westelm.com

Many of West Elm's most popular lines reflect key features of mid-century modern style; 50 retail outlets nationwide.

YOUNGER FURNITURE

110 Todd Court
Thomasville, NC 27360

www.youngerfurniture.com

The Avenue 62 collection consists of new pieces inspired by the style of the 1950s, 1960s and 1970s.

PICTURE CREDITS

1 Jo Shane, John Cooper and family, apartment in New York. Photography by Andrew Wood; 2 John Cheim's apartment in New York. Photography by Andrew Wood; 3 left Photography by Hans Hansen. Wire Chair DKR-2 Design Charles & Ray Eames, 1951 © Vitra Collections AG; 3 centre Photography by Andreas Sütterlin. ESU Bookcase, Design Charles & Ray Eames, 1949 © Vitra Collections AG; 3 right Design Museum Collection; 4 James Merrell/Jan Staller's house in New York. Photography by Andrew Wood; 5 & 6 Century 020 7487 5100. Photography by Andrew Wood; 7 Photography by Andrew Wood; 8 left Ray Main/Lee F. Mindel's apartment in New York, designed by Shelton, Mindel & Associates with Associate Architect Reed Morrison, lighting designed by Johnson Schwinghammer. Photography by Andrew Wood; 8 right John Cheim's apartment in New York. Photography by Andrew Wood; 9 Michael Benevento – Orange Group. Photography by Andrew Wood; 10 Guido Palau's house in North London, designed by Azman Owens Architects. Photography by Andrew Wood; 11 left Aki Wahlman's summer home in Finland. Photography by Paul Ryan; 11 right Century 020 7487 5100. Photography by Andrew Wood; 12 left © 2013. Digital image, The Museum of Modern Art, New York/Scala, Florence; 12 centre www.vitra.com; 12 right © 2013. Digital image, The Museum of Modern Art, New York/Scala, Florence; 13 left © 2013. Digital image, The Museum of Modern Art, New York/Scala, Florence; 13 centre © Victoria and Albert Museum, London; 13 right courtesy of Iittala, https://www.iittala.com; 14 left www.vitra.com; 14 centre Ant designed by Arne Jacobsen, cherry. www.fritzhansen.com; 14 right Design Museum Collection; 15 left © 2013. Digital image, The Museum of Modern Art, New York/Scala, Florence; 15 centre © Vitra Collections; 15 right Arco designed by Achille and Pier Giacomo Castiglioni for Flos. www.flos.com; 16–17 Neil Bingham's house in Blackheath, London, chair courtesy of Designer's Guild. Photography by Andrew Wood; 18 Ian Chee's apartment in London. Photography by Andrew Wood; 19 above Nigel Smith's loft in London. Photography by Andrew Wood; 19 below The Mogensen family's home in Gentofte, Denmark. Photography by Andrew Wood; 20 above picture courtesy of Nakashima Studio Archives; 20 below and 21 above Photography by Tham Nhu-Tran; 21 below Target Gallery, London. Photography by Thomas Stewart; 22 Heidi Kingstone's apartment in London. Photography by Andrew Wood; 23 above left Guido Palau's house in North London, designed by Azman Owens Architects. Photography by Andrew Wood; 23 above centre Brian Johnson's apartment in London, designed by Johnson Naylor, chairs courtesy of Race Furniture. Photography by Andrew Wood; 23 above right Century 020 7487 5100. Photography by Andrew Wood; 24 The Kjærholms' family home in Rungsted, Denmark. Photography by Andrew Wood; 24 inset The home of Ingegerd Raman and Claes Söderquist in Sweden. Photography by Paul Ryan; 25 left www.ercol.com 01844 271 800; 25 right Coexistence 020 7354 8817. Photography by Andrew Wood; 26 Century 020 7487 5100. Photography by Andrew Wood; 27 Norma Holland's house in London. Photography by Andrew Wood; 28 left Photography by Arnold Brunner © Vitra; 28 right Photographer: Michael Cullen. Courtesy of Knoll, Inc.; 29 Jo Shane, John Cooper and family, apartment in New York. Photography by Andrew Wood; 30 Aki Wahlman's summer home in Finland. Photography by Paul Ryan; 30 inset www.eero-aarnio.com; 31 ©Joshua McHugh. Photo courtesy of Knoll, Inc.; 32 Guido Palau's house in North London, designed by Azman Owens Architects. Photography by Andrew Wood; 33 Heidi Kingstone's apartment in London. Photography by Andrew Wood; 34 Stephen Shayler and Stephen Worth's house in Brighton. Photography by Thomas Stewart; 35 above Annette Main and Justin De Syllas' house in London, chair courtesy of Fritz Hansen. Photography by Andrew Wood; below Courtesy of Robert Welch Designs Archive; 36 left Photography by Thomas Stewart; 36 right Target Gallery, London. Photography by Thomas Stewart; 37 An apartment in The San Remo on the Upper West Side of Manhattan, designed by John L. Stewart and Michael D'Arcy of SIT. Photography by Andrew Wood; 38 left Chelsea Loft apartment in new York, designed by The Modern. Photography by Andrew Wood; 38 right John Cheim's apartment in New York. Photography by Andrew Wood; 39 above Century 020 7487 5100. Photography by Andrew Wood; 39 below Photography by Tam Nhu Tran/Ian Chee's apartment in London; 40 Peter Holmblad's apartment in Klampenborg, Denmark, designed by architect Arne Jacobsen in 1958. Photography by Andrew Wood; 41 above Courtesy of Nat Davies and Guinevere Antiques; 41 below Image Courtesy of Knoll, Inc.; 42 above Furnishing fabric (printed cotton), Whitehead, David (20th century) / Private Collection / The Bridgeman Art Library; 42 below © David L. Moore / Alamy; 43 Ray Main / Mainstream Images / David Gill; 44 The home of Ellen Weiman & Dubi Silverstein in New York, designed by Architects Ogawa / Depardon. Photography by Andrew Wood; 45 An apartment in The San Remo on the Upper West Side of Manhattan, designed by John L. Stewart and Michael D'Arcy of SIT. Photography by Andrew Wood; 46 inset Photography by Tham Nhu-Tran; Pages 46–47 Candelabra from Boom. Photography by Thomas Stewart; 48 An original Florida home restored by Andrew Weaving of Century, www.centuryd.com. Photography by Andrew Wood; 49 Photography by Marc Eggimann © Vitra; 50 left The house of Greta & David Iredale in Surrey. Photography by Andrew Wood; 50 above right Marcus Hewitt and Susan Hooper's home in Litchfield County, Connecticut. Photography by Debi Treloar; 50 below right An original Florida home restored by Andrew Weaving of Century, www.centuryd.com. Photography by Andrew Wood; 51 An original Florida home restored by Andrew Weaving of Century, www.centuryd.com. Photography by Andrew Wood; 52 Photography by Tam Nhu Tran / Ian Chee's apartment in London; 53 An apartment in The San Remo on the Upper West Side of Manhattan, designed by John L. Stewart and Michael D'Arcy of SIT. Photography by Andrew Wood; 54 above Marshmallow sofa designed by George Nelson manufactured by Vitra © Vitra; 54 below The Paris apartment of Nicolas Hug. Photography by Andrew Wood; 55 Ian Chee's apartment in London, chair courtesy of Vitra. Photography by Andrew Wood; 56 © Victoria and Albert Museum, London; 57 left Photography by Andrew Wood; 57 right © Victoria and Albert Museum, London; 58 left Target Gallery, London. Photography by Thomas Stewart; right Photography by Andrew Wood; below Photography by Tham Nhu-Tran; Pages 59 and 60 © Victoria and Albert Museum, London; 61 Yuen-Wei Chew's apartment in London designed by Paul Daly represented by Echo Design Agency. Photography by Thomas Stewart; 62 above and centre Photography by Tham Nhu-Tran; below Courtesy of Modernity – www.modernity.se; 63 Svenskt Tenn / design by Josef Frank; 64 Photography by Andrew Wood; 65 www.1stdibs.com; 66 Photography by Tham Nhu-Tran; 67 above © Victoria and Albert Museum, London; 67 below Photography by René Riis; 68 above left Photography by Hans Hansen. © Vitra; 68 above right www.1stdibs.com; 68 below Glass courtesy of Skandium. Photography by Thomas Stewart; 69 Television from Places and Spaces. Photography by Thomas Stewart; 70 and 71 right Eero Aarnio's house in Veikkola. Finland. Photography by Andrew Wood; 71 left Apartment of Michel Hurst / Robert Swope, owners of Full House NYC. Photography by Andrew Wood; 72–73 Photography by Andrew Wood; 74 Nigel Smith's loft in London. Photography by Andrew Wood; 75 Jeff Priess and Rebecca Quaytman's apartment in New York designed by Fernlund and Logan Architects. Photography by Andrew Wood; 76 The home of stylist Emma Persson Lagerberg. Photography by Polly Wreford; 77 left © Pastoe; 77 right Paul Massey / Naja Lauf; 78 left Ignazia Favata – Studio Joe Colombo Milano; 78 right Image Courtesy of Knoll, Inc.; 79 Annette Main and Justin De Syllas' house

in London, chairs courtesy of Hille UK. Photography by Andrew Wood; **80**; Brian Johnson's apartment in London, designed by Johnson Naylor, chairs courtesy of Race Furniture. Photography by Andrew Wood; **81 left** Nigel Smith's loft in London. Photography by Andrew Wood; **81 right** Brian Johnson's apartment in London, designed by Johnson Naylor. Photography by Andrew Wood; **82** The family home of Nina Tolstrup and Jack Mama of www.studiomama.com. Photography by Debi Treloar; **83** Coexistence 020 7354 8817. Photography by Andrew Wood; **84 above left** The Mogensen family's home in Gentofte, Denmark. Photography by Andrew Wood; **84 above right** www.1stdibs.com; **84 below** An apartment in Knokke, Belgium designed by Claire Bataille and Paul Ibens. Photography by Andrew Wood; **85 left** Phillip Low, New York. Photography by Andrew Wood; **85 right** Photography by Andrew Wood; **86 left** The loft of Peggy & Steven Learner, designed by Steven Learner Studio. Photography by Andrew Wood; **87** Jo Shane, John Cooper and family, apartment in New York. Photography by Andrew Wood; **88 above** Photography by Andrew Wood; **88 below** Hans Hansen © Vitra; **89 above** Image Courtesy of Knoll, Inc; **89 below** Photography by Andrew Wood; **90 above** Frédéric Méchiche's apartment in Paris. Photography by Fritz von der Schulenburg; **90 below** The Mogensen family's home in Gentofte, Denmark. Photography by Andrew Wood; **91 above** An apartment in The San Remo on the Upper West Side of Manhattan, designed by John L. Stewart and Michael D'Arcy of SIT. Photography by Andrew Wood; **91 below** Apartment of Michel Hurst / Robert Swope, owners of Full House NYC. Photography by Andrew Wood; **92 above** Jeff Priess and Rebecca Quaytman's apartment in New York designed by Fernlund and Logan Architects. Photography by Andrew Wood; **92 below** Theban daybed by Ferdinand Kramer, re-editioned by e15. Image © e15; **93** Michael Benevento – Orange Group. Photography by Andrew Wood; **94 and 95 left** Heidi Kingstone's apartment in London. Photography by Andrew Wood; **95 right** Century 020 7487 5100. Photography by Andrew Wood; **95 below** Image Courtesy of Knoll, Inc.; **96** above Aki Wahlman's summer home in Finland. Photography by Paul Ryan; **96** below www.ercol.com 01844 271 800; **97** Jo Shane, John Cooper and family, apartment in New York. Photography by Andrew Wood; **98** The Alexander home of Bruce Mink in Palm Springs. Photography by Andrew Wood; **99** An original Florida home restored by Andrew Weaving of Century, www.centuryd.com. Photography by Andrew Wood; **Pages 100–101** Photography by Andrew Wood; **102** Photography by Andrew Wood; **103** above An apartment in The San Remo on the Upper West Side of Manhattan, designed by John L. Stewart and Michael D'Arcy of SIT. Photography by Andrew Wood; **103 below** Calvert and FK05 Charlotte side tables by Ferdinand Kramer, re-editioned by e15 Image © e15; **104 above** Image Courtesy of Knoll, Inc.; **104** Kurt Bredenbeck's apartment at the Barbican, London. Photography by Andrew Wood; **105** John Edward Linden/ Arcaid Images; **106** Century 0207 487 5100. Photography by Andrew Wood; **107 left** © Victoria and Albert Museum, London; **107 right** Aki Wahlman's summer home in Finland. Photography by Paul Ryan; **108 left** An apartment in The San Remo on the Upper West Side of Manhattan, designed by John L. Stewart and Michael D'Arcy of SIT. Photography by Andrew Wood; **108 right** Photography by Andrew Wood; **109** Camera Press / Hemis / Dominique Vorillon; **110–111** The London Loft of Andrew Weaving of Century, www.centuryd.com. Photography by Andrew Wood; **112** Photography by Andrew Wood; **113 above left** Apartment of Michel Hurst / Robert Swope, owners of Full House NYC. Photography by Andrew Wood; **113 above right** Phillip Low, New York. Photography by Andrew Wood; **113 below** Snoopy designed by Achille and Pier Giacomo Castiglioni for Flos. www.flos.com; **114 above left** Jane Collins of Sixty 6 home in central London. Photography by Andrew Wood; **114 above right** Justin De Syllas, light courtesy of Skandium. Photography by Chris Everard; **114 below** The Paris apartment of Nicolas Hug. Photography by Andrew Wood; **115** Frédéric Méchiche's apartment in Paris. Photography by Fritz von der Schulenburg; **116** Nanna Ditzel's home in Copenhagen. Photography by Andrew Wood; **117 left** Photographer Ray Main; **117 right** Nanna Ditzel's home in Copenhagen. Photography by Andrew Wood; **118 above left** © Louis Poulsen; **118 above right** www.verpan.com; **118 below left** Chelsea Loft apartment in New York, designed by The Moderns. Photography by Andrew Wood; **119** Guido Palau's house in North London, designed by Azman Owens Architects. Photography by Andrew Wood; **119 inset** Photographer Ray Main; **120** Jane Collins of Sixty 6 in Marylebone High Street, home in central London. Photography by Andrew Wood; **121** © Marimekko Corporation; **122** Photography by Andrew Wood; **123** Neil Bingham's house in Blackheath, London. Photography by Thomas Stewart; **Pages 124–125** Photography by Andrew Wood; **126** Century 020 7487 5100. Photography by Andrew Wood; **127 above** www.1stdibs.com; **127 below** Bitossi Ceramiche; **Pages 128–129** Brian Johnson's apartment in London, designed by Johnson Naylor. Photography by Tam Nhu Tran; **128 inset** Stephen Shayler and Stephen Worth's house in Brighton. Photography by Thomas Stewart; **130 left** Stephen Shayler and Stephen Worth's house in Brighton. Photography by Thomas Stewart; **131 both right and 131 above** Courtesy of Modernity – www.modernity.se; **131 below** The Museum of Modern Art, New York / Scala, Florence; **132 below left** Collection of The Corning Museum of Glass, Corning, New York; **132 above** Collection of The Corning Museum of Glass, Corning, New York, gift of The Steinberg Foundation; **132 below right** Jane Collins of Sixty 6 in Marylebone High Street, home in central London. Photography by Andrew Wood; **133** An apartment in The San Remo on the Upper West Side of Manhattan, designed by John L. Stewart and Michael D'Arcy of SIT. Photography by Andrew Wood; **134** Stephen Shayler and Stephen Worth's house in Brighton. Photography by Thomas Stewart; **135 left** http://www.orrefors.com; **135 above right** www.ronaldstennettwillson.com; **135 below** Ceramic dishes courtesy of Gary Grant Choice Pieces. Photography by Thomas Stewart; **136 left** Photography by Thomas Stewart; **136 right** Collection of The Corning Museum of Glass, Corning, New York **137** Courtesy of Gary Grant Choice Pieces. Photography by Thomas Stewart; **138** Target Gallery, London. Photography by Thomas Stewart; **139** Ron Wigham & Rachel Harding's apartment in London. Photography by Thomas Stewart; **140 above** David Mellor Design; **140 below** www.georgjensen.com; **141** The Goldsmiths' Company; **142 above** www.georgjensen.com; below left The Goldsmiths' Company; below right David Mellor Design; **143 left** The Goldsmiths' Company; **143 right** David Mellor Design; **144–145** The Finn Juhl house in Charlottenlund, Denmark. Photography by Andrew Wood. Today Finn Juhl's house is a museum and part of Ordrupgaard. It is open to the public on weekends from 11am–4:45pm. In June, July and August Tuesday 1–4:45 pm; Wednesday 1–6:45 pm, Friday 1–4:45pm. http://ordrupgaard.dk/topics/collection-and-architecture/finn-juhl's-house.aspx; **146–151** Media executive's house in Los Angeles. Architect: Stephen Slan. Builder: Ken Duran. Furnishings: Russel Simpson. Original Architect: Carl Matson c.1945. Photography by Andrew Wood; **152–163** Century 020 7487 5100. Photography by Andrew Wood; **164–171** Photographer Prue Ruscoe/Taverne Agency. Producer: Andrea Millar; **172–177** Interior designer Philip Hooper's house in East Sussex. Photography by Jan Baldwin; **178–189** Photographer and Producer; Ngoc Minh Ngo / Taverne Agency; **190–197** The Finn Juhl house in Charlottenlund, Denmark. Photography by Andrew Wood. Today Finn Juhl's house is a museum and part of Ordrupgaard. It is open to the public on weekends from 11am–4:45pm. In June, July and August Tuesday 1pm–4:45 pm; Wednesday 1pm–6:45 pm, Friday 1pm–4:45pm as well. http://ordrupgaard.dk/topics/collection-and-architecture/finn-juhl's-house.aspx; **198–207** The home of Sean and Tricia Brunson in Orlando. Photography by Andrew Wood; **208** Anna & John Carver. Photography by Polly Wreford; **209 left** Kurt Bredenbeck's apartment at the Barbican, London. Photography by Andrew Wood; **209 right** image courtesy of www.modernshows.com; **210 above** Evan Snyderman's house in Brooklyn. Photography by Ray Main; **210 below** image courtesy of www.modernshows.com; **211** The Paris apartment of Nicolas Hug. Photography by Andrew Wood; **212** The home of Andy Marcus and Ron Diliberto in Palm Springs. Photography by Andrew Wood; **213 above** Coffee service courtesy of Rosenthal. Photography by Thomas Stewart; **213 below** image courtesy of www.modernshows.com.

BUSINESS CREDITS

The following companies kindly lent us images for inclusion in this book:

1STDIBS
www.1stdibs.com
Jorgen Hovelskov's Harp chair, Piero Fornasetti furniture, Olivier Mourgue seating and West German 'Fat lava' vases.

ARIA
Barnsbury Hall
Barnsbury Street
London N1 1PN, UK
020 7704 6222
www.ariashop.co.uk
Bitossi Blu Rimini ceramics.

BITOSSI CERAMICHE
Via A. Gramschi16
50056 Montelupo Fiorentino,
Florence, Italy
+ 39 0571 51403
www.bitossiceramiche.it
Bitossi Blu Rimini ceramics.

DAVID MELLOR
The Round Building
Hathersage
Sheffield S32 1BA, UK
01433 650220
www.davidmellordesign.co.uk
David Mellor cutlery.

ERCOL
Summerleys Road
Princes Risborough
Bucks HP27 9PX, UK
01844 271800
www.ercol.com
Manufacturers of the Ercol Loveseat and Butterfly chair.

FLOS
7–15 Rosebery Avenue
London EC1R 4SP, UK
020 3328 5140
www.flos.com
Achille and Giacomo Castiglioni Arco and Snoopy lights.

GEORG JENSEN
15 New Bond Street
London W1S 3ST, UK
020 7499 6541
www.georgjensen.com
Arne Jacobsen cutlery and Henning Koppel silverware, both for Georg Jensen.

GEORGE NAKASHIMA
Woodworker SA
1847 Aquetong Road
New Hope, PA 18938, USA
215-862-2272
www.nakashimawoodworker.com
George Nakashima furniture.

GUINEVERE ANTIQUES
574–580 King's Road
London SW6 2DY, UK
020 7736 2917
www.guinevere.co.uk
Paul Evans furniture.

KNOLL
91 Goswell Rd,
London EC1V 7EX, UK
020 7236 6655
www.knoll-int.com
Florence Knoll, Eero Saarinen, Harry Bertoia, Warren Platner and George Nakashima furniture.

THE LONDON SILVER VAULTS
Chancery House
53–64 Chancery Lane
London WC2A 1QS, UK
020 7242 3844
www.thesilvervaults.com
and

STYLES SILVER
12 Bridge Street
Hungerford
Berkshire RG17 0EH, UK
01488 683922
www.styles-silver.co.uk
Stuart Devlin metalware.

SELFRIDGES, SKANDIUM
400 Oxford Street
London W1A 1AB, UK
020 7318 3379
www.selfridges.com
Orrefors glassware.

SKANDIUM
245–249 Brompton Road
London SW3 2EP, UK
020 7584 2066
www.skandium.com
Tapio Wirkkala glassware for Iittala, Poul Henningsen lighting for Louis Poulsen, Marimekko and Stig Lindberg fabrics, Orrefors glassware.

SIGMAR
263 King's Road,
London SW3 5EL, UK
020 7751 5801
www.sigmarlondon.com
Finn Juhl and Hans Wegner furniture.

RONALD STENNETT-WILLSON
www.ronaldstennettwillson.com

SVENSKT TENN
www.svenskttenn.se
Josef Frank fabrics.

VERPAN
00 45 76581882
www.verpan.com
Verner Panton lighting

VIADUCT
1–10 Summers Street
London EC1R 5BD, UK
020 7278 8456
www.viaduct.co.uk
Ferdinand Kramer furniture re-editions by e15 and Cees Braakman chair for Pastoe.

VITRA
30 Clerkenwell Road
London EC1M 5PG, UK
020 7608 6200
www.vitra.com
Charles and Ray Eames, George Nelson and Verner Panton furniture and homeware, Isamu Noguchi lighting and Alexander Girard Wooden Dolls for Vitra.

ROBERT WELCH DESIGNS
Lower High Street
Chipping Campden
Gloucestershire GL55 6DY, UK
01386 840522
www.robertwelch.com
Robert Welch metalware.

With special thanks to:

THE CORNING MUSEUM OF GLASS
http://www.cmog.org

THE FINN JUHL HOUSE, DENMARK
www.ordrupgaard.dk
The Finn Juhl house in Charlottenlund, Denmark is now a museum and part of Ordrupgaard. Please visit the website for details of opening hours.

HILLE
www.hille.co.uk

MODERNITY
www.modernity.se

THE NOGUCHI MUSEUM
32–37 Vernon Boulevard
Long Island City, NY 11106, USA
718-204-7088
www.noguchi.org

TRAQUAIR
www.traquair.1stdibs.com
07702 495689

BIBLIOGRAPHY

Neil Bingham and Andrew Weaving,
*Modern Retro: Living with
Mid-Century Modern Style*
(Ryland, Peters & Small, 2005)

Steven Braggs and Basil Hyman,
*The G-Plan Revolution:
A Celebration of British Popular
Furniture of the 1950s and 1960s*
(Booth-Clibborn Editions, 2007

Richard Chamberlain, Geoffrey
Rayner and Annemarie Stapleton,
*Jacqueline Groag, Textile &
Pattern Design: Wiener Werkstätte
to American Modern*
(Antique Collectors' Club, 2009)

Cara Greenberg,
*Mid-Century Modern –
Furniture from the 1950s*
(Thames & Hudson, 1985)

Bevis Hillier,
The Style of the Century, 1900-1980
(The Herbert Press, 1983)

Lesley Jackson,
*Contemporary: Architecture and
Interiors of the 1950s*
(Phaidon, 1994)

Lesley Jackson,
The New Look: Design in the Fifties
(Thames & Hudson, 1991)

Judith Miller,
Chairs
(Conran Octopus, 2009)

Judith Miller,
*Mid-Century Modern: Living
with Mid-Century Modern Design*
(Miller's, 2012)

Penny Sparke,
*A Century of Design: Design
Pioneers of the 20th Century*
(Mitchell Beazley, 1998)

Jonathan M. Woodham,
Oxford Dictionary of Modern Design
(Oxford University Press, 2004)

BLOGS

AQUA VELVET
Stylish, intriguingly esoteric site
showcasing mid-century houses,
art, graphics, logos, Polish posters
and Japanese illustration.
www.aqua-velvet.com

DESIGN SPONGE
Site showcasing stylish mid-century
and mid-century-inspired homes
and design.
www.designsponge.com

GRAIN EDIT
This focuses on 1950s to 1970s graphics
and illustration and their influence on
contemporary designers.
http://grainedit.com

LUSHPAD
US site that sells mid-century furniture
and features collecting tips, designer
biographies and mid-century-related
news.
www.lushpad.com
www.lushpad.com/blog

MARK HILL PUBLISHING
Website and blog of Mark Hill, presenter
of BBC Television's Antiques Roadshow,
author and dealer in postwar Czech glass.
www.markhillpublishing.com
www.markhillpublishing.com/blog

MID-CENTURIA
Features mid-century art, design and
interiors, and similar subjects.
www.midcenturia.com

THE MIDCENTURY MODERN SHOWS
These shows' organizers have four
websites and/or blogs, as follows:
www.modernshows.com
Information on Midcentury Modern's
various exhibitions and pop-up shops.

www.midcenturymodernmarketplace.com
An extensive sourcing directory for people
passionate about 20th-century design,
including mid-century.

www.insidemodernism.co.uk
A blog with contributions from the
organizers, participants and fans of the
Midcentury Modern shows.

www.destinationmodernism.com
A travel blog for architecture tourists
who love mid-century style.

THE MID-CENTURY MODERNIST
Stephen Coles's website celebrates all
areas of mid-century design and its
influence on contemporary culture.
www.midcenturymodernist.com

MODERN FINDINGS
This blog includes directories of mid-
century shops, the blogger's mid-century
collection and related items.
www.modernfindings.com

MONDO BLOGO
Blog with a highly personal selection of
design and architecture including mid-
century houses.
mondo-blogo.blogspot.co.uk

PLASTOLUX
An architecture and design site that
showcases mid-century houses and mid-
century-inspired new architecture.
www.plastolux.com

MID-CENTURY HOME
Site that brims with information about
important mid-century designs – a great
resource for collectors.
www.www.mid-century-home.com

QUAD ROYAL
A blog that celebrates British postwar
graphics and posters, including for Shell
and London Transport.
www.vintageposterblog.com

RETRO TO GO
This site is packed with mid-century and
pop design and contemporary design
inspired by both.
www.retrotogo.com

RETROWOW
An online 'information resource' about
design and fashion from the 1930s to
the 1990s.
www.retrowow.co.uk

THE HOUSE OF TOMORROW
Website advertising stylish mid-century
houses and bungalows for sale.
www.thehouseoftomorrow.co.uk

TRIANGLE MODERNIST HOUSES
US site with massive pictorial archive of
mid-century modern architecture in the
US and elsewhere.
www.trianglemodernisthouses.com

THE VINTAGE FESTIVAL
Website and blog of the UK-wide Vintage
Festival, which celebrates 20th-century
design, fashion and music.
www.vintagefestival.co.uk
www.vintagefestival.co.uk/eventsBlog

WOWHAUS
Website that flags up swanky, modernist,
20th-century properties on the market,
many by well-known architects.
www.wowhaus.co.uk

INDEX

ACKNOWLEDGMENTS

My special thanks to my partner Chris Bourne, to my parents Beatriz and Martin Lutyens and my friend and fellow mid-century fan Nicole Polonsky for all their support and encouragement.

Thanks to those who kindly agreed to be interviewed, in particular to Simon Andrews for his scholarly overview of mid-century design and to Corinne Julius for her fascinating eyewitness accounts of postwar Britain's avant-garde design milieu. I'm also grateful to Lucy Ryder Richardson and Petra Curtis for their help – including providing images from their archive – as well as Charlotte Abrahams, Soomi Amagasu, Eleni Bide, Sean Brunson, Helen Desai, Clare Dowdy, Belinda Fisher, Chris Green, Wayne Hemingway, Nina Hertig, Philip Hooper, Clare Hulton, Pippa Kahn, James Lawless, Marcos Lutyens, Emma McNiven, Zoe Ramsay, Hugo Rawlins, Jefferson Smith, Amanda Stücklin, Andrew Weaving, Julienne Webster and Anna Wilcox.

My thanks, too, to the Ryland Peters & Small team: commissioning editor Annabel Morgan, picture editor Christina Borsi and designer Paul Tilby.